WHAT WE VALUE

THE MALCOLM LESTER PHI BETA KAPPA LECTURES
ON THE LIBERAL ARTS AND PUBLIC LIFE
EDITED BY DAVID A. DAVIS

WHAT WE VALUE

Public Health, Social Justice, and
Educating for Democracy

LYNN PASQUERELLA

UNIVERSITY OF VIRGINIA PRESS
Charlottesville and London

University of Virginia Press
© 2022 by the Rector and Visitors of the University of Virginia
All rights reserved
Printed in the United States of America on acid-free paper

First published 2022
First paperback edition published 2023
ISBN 978-0-8139-4996-3 (paper)

9 8 7 6 5 4 3 2 1

The Library of Congress has cataloged the hardcover edition as follows:

Names: Pasquerella, Lynn, author.
Title: What we value : public health, social justice, and educating for
    democracy / Lynn Pasquerella.
Description: Charlottesville : University of Virginia Press, 2022. | Series: The
    Malcolm Lester Phi Beta Kappa lectures on the liberal arts and public life |
    Includes bibliographical references.
Identifiers: LCCN 2021035857 (print) | LCCN 2021035858 (ebook) |
    ISBN 9780813948478 (hardcover) | ISBN 9780813948485 (ebook)
Subjects: LCSH: Education, Humanistic. | Public health—Moral and
    ethical aspects. | Social justice and education. | COVID-19 (Disease) |
    Democracy—Study and teaching.
Classification: LCC LC1011 .P32 2022 (print) | LCC LC1011 (ebook) |
    DDC 370.11/2—dc23
LC record available at https://lccn.loc.gov/2021035857
LC ebook record available at https://lccn.loc.gov/2021035858

Cover art: Highlighter, mr.kriangsak kitisak/Shutterstock.com; lettering,
Derek Thornton/Notch Design

To Dr. Sam Pope and Dr. Oladunni Filani, for embodying Francis Peabody's adage that "the secret of the care of the patient is in caring for the patient"

CONTENTS

ACKNOWLEDGMENTS

The essays contained in this volume were written during a period of quarantine and lockdown resulting from the COVID-19 pandemic. When the offices of the American Association of Colleges and Universities (AAC&U) closed at the beginning of March 2020 and we transitioned to remote work, I returned to our family home in Woodstock, Connecticut, to be with my husband, John Kuchle. In the more than four decades that we have been married, he has offered constant support—cheering me on throughout my professional life and being all one could hope for in a husband and father to our twin sons, Pierce and Spencer. I learn from him daily, and I am deeply grateful for his enthusiastic response whenever I ask if it would be okay to read him my latest speech, article, or chapter.

Within a few weeks of my settling into life in "the Quiet Corner," we were joined by Spencer, whose AmeriCorps service sites in Appalachia were temporarily shut down, and by my sister, Keli, and her husband, Peter, whose businesses were placed on hiatus. I could not have asked for better companions for late-night conversations, corn hole, pool matches, and board games. The stress and uncertainty of the seemingly endless days were mitigated by being with caring, fun-loving, and intellectually stimulating individuals during a time when we all came to realize that health and family mean more than anything. I am truly grateful for all they did to make my work possible.

Although Pierce was not with us, I deeply appreciate the enormous contributions he made to my finishing this manuscript by using his skills as a cinematographer to ensure that I was able to connect with our members digitally while remaining safe at home.

In addition, I want to thank my inspirational colleagues at AAC&U and at the Phi Beta Kappa Society for their extraordinary commitment to championing liberal education, the free exchange of ideas, and quality and equity in higher education. I was honored to receive the invitation from David Davis to deliver the 2020 Malcolm Lester Lectures at Mercer University, and his leadership in furthering the values of the Society has been exemplary. Thanks also to Eric Brandt, Ellen Satrom, and Helen Chandler from the University of Virginia Press for their guidance, support, and encouragement throughout this project.

Finally, whenever I am up at night, going over in my mind the most vexing philosophical conundrums, I turn to Professor Cheryl Foster, from the University of Rhode Island, and Secretary Frederick Lawrence, CEO of Phi Beta Kappa. The keen analytical ability, wit, and wisdom they display is matched only by their integrity. I hope they know how profoundly I cherish their friendship and their extraordinary contributions to excellence in liberal education.

FOREWORD

Mercer University hosts the Malcolm Lester Phi Beta Kappa Lectures on the Liberal Arts and Public Life each year as part of our Phi Beta Kappa induction ceremony. The lectures allow our students to meet an important figure in American higher education and to have conversations about the value of the liberal arts. This experience reinforces the significance of the students' accomplishment in being inducted into Phi Beta Kappa, and the conversations can be inspiring, but a series of lectures and conversations among a small group of people has a limited effect. Dr. Malcolm Lester had a vision for a series of lectures that supports the mission of the Phi Beta Kappa Society and that reaches a broad audience to influence the discourse about liberal arts in the United States.

Dr. Malcolm Lester graduated from Mercer in 1945, and he returned to Mercer after graduate school to teach history. He was named dean of the College of Liberal Arts and Sciences in 1955, and in 1959, he left Mercer to join the faculty of Davidson College, where he taught for the next thirty years. While at Davidson, he served as a Phi Beta Kappa senator and member of the Committee on Qualifications, which reviews schools' applications to shelter chapters of the Phi Beta Kappa Society. He felt strongly that Mercer should also shelter a chapter of Phi Beta Kappa, and he encouraged faculty to apply. In 2007, he made a gift for a lecture series on the liberal arts at Mercer to commence once

Mercer sheltered a chapter of the Phi Beta Kappa Society, and Mercer received a charter in 2016. His bequest states that "the income of such endowed fund shall be used to pay for the delivery of and publication of an annual oration to be delivered by a distinguished scholar at the annual initiation of members in course of Phi Beta Kappa." The lectures are published by the University of Virginia Press, as requested by Dr. Lester, who earned his Ph.D. from the University of Virginia, where he was inducted into Phi Beta Kappa as a graduate student.

The 2020 lectures were scheduled for March. In January 2020, a novel coronavirus entered the United States, disrupting most aspects of daily life. The deadly pathogen was passed by respiratory excretions, which made gathering in large groups dangerous, and it progressed rapidly across the country with high rates of infection and shocking rates of mortality. Institutions of higher education, like all other enterprises, scrambled to respond to the pandemic. By the end of February, most institutions had canceled in-person classes, rearranged syllabuses, sent students home, and turned to online technology to deliver instruction. The Lester Lectures, like many other ordinary events, were postponed as Mercer grappled with the pandemic on campus. By August 2020, universities had developed protocols for managing the virus. Many schools continued to use online instruction; some, including Mercer, returned to face-to-face classes with elaborate public health measures in place; and others offered hybrid options that blended in-person classes with virtual courses. The lectures were rescheduled for September and, like many other events, delivered over Zoom.

The pandemic was an inflection point for higher education that simultaneously amplified underlying challenges and revealed institutional values. Going into 2020, many colleges and universities still contended with reduced funding levels extending back to the 2008 economic crisis, and some institutions were experiencing declines in overall enrollment that led to the closure of several smaller tuition-dependent schools. Liberal arts disciplines, meanwhile, continue to experience lagging majors as students gravitate toward more presumably lucrative vocational fields, which has led to the downsizing and closure of some liberal arts departments at colleges across the country. Contempt from politicians and state legislators, who sometimes question the utility of liberal arts majors, and concern from parents and students about the cost of a liberal arts degree have added pressure on institutions struggling to maintain their viability.

The pandemic amplified these pressures. The abrupt pivot to online instruction in the spring of 2020 created a ripple of challenges that increased costs, reduced revenue, disrupted the learning environment, taxed faculty resources, and placed students in academic jeopardy. All of these problems endured through the 2020–21 academic year, leading to declines in new student enrollment and international student enrollment, pay cuts and furloughs for faculty and staff members at many institutions, reductions in revenue from tuition and fees, suspension of international programs, and disruptions to college athletics. These challenges have stressed institutional budgets and negatively affected the student experience at schools across the country.

Teaching and learning through a crisis have also revealed the fundamental values of higher education. As institutions grappled with challenges and disruptions, the top priority for most schools was how to protect student safety while delivering quality instruction. Schools implemented a range of procedures to achieve these goals, and they were successful for the most part. Despite enormous pressures, courses were delivered, most students made progress, and classes graduated. Many students, however, struggled with mental health issues and financial challenges, and others deferred or delayed higher education, at least for a while. As the pandemic subsides, many questions linger about how institutions of higher education will change as a result of the crisis and how they might reevaluate their mission going forward.

Higher education faces enormous challenges at this moment, and the Lester Lectures committee selected the ideal person to address these issues. We chose Dr. Lynn Pasquerella, a person who has devoted her career to addressing issues of accessibility and quality in the liberal arts. Dr. Pasquerella is president of the American Association of Colleges and Universities and immediate past president of the Phi Beta Kappa Society. A graduate of Quinebaug Valley Community College, Mount Holyoke College, and Brown University, where she earned a Ph.D. in philosophy, she taught at the University of Rhode Island and served as provost of the University of Hartford and as president of Mount Holyoke College. As a scholar, she has received major grants to study the ethics of the Human Genome Project and to promote the careers of women in STEM fields in addition to other projects. She has served on the boards of major organizations and has received numerous awards, including several honorary doctorates. She also hosts *The Academic Minute* on public radio. As a scholar, administrator, and advocate, she understands the complexity of the issues higher education currently faces.

In *What We Value*, Dr. Pasquerella demonstrates how liberal education prepares students to respond to moments of crisis by examining three test cases that demonstrate how free inquiry and critical thinking promote ethical decision-making. She first addresses how Americans regard death, an issue exacerbated by the pandemic, and she explains the moral distress that physicians endure as they negotiate end-of-life issues. Next, she discusses the politicization of free speech on college campuses, which became highly contentious in the previous presidential administration, and she explains why free speech is valuable even when it is unpopular. Then, she analyzes the role of liberal education in post-truth political discourse, in which rampant charges of "fake news" and the proffering of "alternative facts," along with massive misinformation campaigns, have challenged our nation's collective ability to understand and process information. In this environment, critical thinking skills are more important than ever to find meaning, make decisions, and rebuild civil discourse.

The Malcolm Lester Lectures provide an important platform for thought leaders in the liberal arts, such as Dr. Pasquerella, to articulate the role of the liberal arts in public life. The Phi Beta Kappa Society is a leading organization advocating for the value and benefits of liberal arts and sciences education, fostering freedom of thought, and recognizing academic excellence, and the Lester Lectures reinforce the Society's mission to advocate for the liberal arts. Many people likely see the value of the liberal arts as self-evident, but the social and political opposition to liberal education indicates that we need to explain how liberal education works, why it matters, and how people benefit from it. The Lester Lectures offer important contributions to the ongoing discourse about the liberal arts and public life, and we are grateful for our partnership with the University of Virginia Press to make this possible.

DAVID A. DAVIS

WHAT WE VALUE

INTRODUCTION

On a sunny October day, about a mile and a half from my home in Washington, D.C., twenty thousand chairs sat empty on the Ellipse, a fifty-three-acre park just south of the White House. Each chair represented ten Americans killed by the novel coronavirus in the nine months following the Trump administration's declaration of COVID-19 as a public health emergency in the United States. At the time, the president himself was at the Walter Reed Army Medical Center being treated for the virus, in the wake of a gathering held at the Rose Garden to introduce Supreme Court nominee Amy Coney Barrett—a reception resulting in at least thirty-four of the two hundred attendees testing positive for COVID-19.

The moving installation at the Ellipse, also called President's Park South, was part of a national day of remembrance organized by COVID Survivors for Change, a network to support those impacted by the coronavirus. The event, which was broadcast virtually, featured musical performances, speakers, and memorial tributes by relatives and friends who had come together not only to mourn but also to call for a national strategy with strong leadership to prevent another two hundred thousand deaths. Grammy Award–winner Dionne Warwick served as the host and highlighted the disproportionate toll the pandemic has taken on Black, Latinx, and Native American communities, alongside the need to acknowledge the ways in which individuals from these groups are often frontline essential workers who have kept the nation fed, housed, and educated. Standing in the background as Warwick spoke was Brian Walter, an attendee whose mask bore the words, "I lost my father. I wear this mask to protect yours. #notjustanumber"—a message reflecting the pain and frustration of those who have lost loved ones and for whom life has been irrevocably changed.[1]

That same week, a plot to kidnap Governor Gretchen Whitmer of Michigan was uncovered by the Federal Bureau of Investigation. In April, protestors wielding guns, wearing bulletproof vests, and demanding an end to stay-at-home orders attempted to storm the state capitol. Many carried Confederate flags and nooses, accompanied by signs comparing the governor to Adolf Hitler and admonishing, "Tyrants Get the Rope." Two weeks earlier, President Trump issued a call to action in a series of tweets encouraging his readers to "Liberate Minnesota," "Liberate Michigan," and "Liberate Virginia." These followed a push by the president to reopen the country by Easter, despite Dr. Anthony Fauci, the White House's infectious diseases expert, asserting that slowing the rate of infection would require several more weeks of aggressive action that would prevent a return to normal. On March 23, 2020, President Trump tweeted, in caps, "WE CANNOT LET THE CURE BE WORSE THAN THE PROBLEM. AT THE END OF THE 15 DAY PERIOD, WE WILL MAKE A DECISION AS TO WHICH WAY WE WANT TO GO!"

Almost immediately, posts appeared on Facebook calling for Governor Whitmer to be beaten, killed, and beheaded. And when thirteen violent extremists from a militia cell, the Wolverine Watchmen, were arrested on charges ranging from conspiracy to kidnap to material support for terrorist acts and carrying or possessing a firearm during the commission of a felony, critics decried the president for inciting violence. After surveillance revealed that the group planned to kidnap Whitmer, place her on trial for treason, and execute her for perceived crimes, the governor issued a press statement about the president's role, saying, "Each time he has tweeted about me, each time that he has said 'liberate Michigan' and said I should negotiate with the very people who are arrested because they're 'good people,' that incites more domestic terror." She went on to argue: "When our leaders speak, their words matter. They carry weight when our leaders meet with, encourage, or fraternize with domestic terrorists. They legitimize their actions, and they are complicit. When they contribute to hate speech, they are complicit."[2]

In response, the White House press secretary, Kayleigh McEnany, accused Governor Whitmer of fueling divisiveness, insisting: "President Trump has continually condemned white supremacists and all forms of hate. Gov. Whitmer is sowing division by making these outlandish allegations. America stands united against hate and in support of our federal law enforcement who stopped this plot."[3] These radically different perspectives on both the appropriate response to the coronavirus pandemic and the limits of free speech in a democratic society that is rife with disinformation campaigns and "troll armies" reflect fundamental intercultural conflicts in America. The cultural battleground is one in which individualism, characterized by personal liberty, is pitted against calls for individual sacrifice for the common good. Amid these partisan divides, the simple acts of wearing masks and engaging in social distancing became flashpoints.

This is not the first time, of course, that Americans have been called upon to restrict their liberties for the welfare of the nation. I remember breezing through airport security with a briefcase containing a bottle of water, a grapefruit, grapefruit knife, and knitting needles, packed on top of books to read and papers to grade. I can also recall sitting cross-legged on the floor in my grandparents' living room, looking through a scrapbook and asking them why they had a "Sugar Book" for rationed sugar, gasoline, butter, and canned milk. In the face of a common enemy following 9/11 and the attack on Pearl Harbor, it went without saying that Americans would accept the curtailing of liberties and engage in sacrifice for the public good.

Today, however, there is no rallying cry against a common enemy. Instead, people living within the same nation appear to be inhabiting two different worlds—some more intent on destroying each other than on vanquishing a deadly virus. The expansiveness of the current divide is exacerbated by a growing populism that has issued forth anti-intellectualism and anti-elitism, signaled by a mistrust of science, the media, government, higher education, and all those who hold divergent points of view. Moreover, it is a divide that, during this moment of crisis, hinders society's ability to address critical questions around whether we can place a price on human life, how to gauge the permissibility of endangering the lives of some for the economic well-being of others, and whether traditional applications of the First Amendment are outmoded in an age of cyberthreats and assault weapons. Overcoming these divisions will depend upon the crucial capacity to speak across differences and identify shared values as a means of restoring mutual trust.

This book's essays explore contemporary controversies centered around what we owe each other as human beings, foregrounding dilemmas that have become more complex and nuanced as a result of the COVID-19 pandemic, the ensuing financial crisis, and this moment of racial reckoning in America. The first, "Moral Distress, Moral Injury, and the Concept of Death as Un-American," examines the impact of COVID-19 on the growing phenomena of moral distress and moral injury among physicians who are being forced to make decisions at odds with their ethical beliefs and commitments as medical professionals.

The urgent necessity to transition from ordinary standards of care that privilege individual autonomy and patients' rights to crisis standards of care relying on a utilitarian ethic led to physicians facing unprecedented challenges. Their medical education has left them ill-prepared for grappling with situations in which they are being asked to allocate scarce resources or engage in the care of patients when it might jeopardize their own health and well-being or that of their families.

If they were fortunate enough to have personal protective equipment, the masks, face shields, and moon suits that offered aegis simultaneously separated them from their patients, imperiling the human connection at the heart of the medical profession. Levels of moral distress exploded as the pandemic magnified health inequities grounded in structural racism, leading to greater uncertainty in ethical decision-making, especially around matters of life and death, and to subsequent feelings of shame, guilt, self-condemnation, and despair.

At the same time, after double shifts, sleepless nights, and separation from their loved ones, many healthcare professionals were forced to navigate a gauntlet of antilockdown protestors who saw them as complicit in an elaborate hoax to destroy the economy. Such scenes have prompted researchers to seek an explanation as to why so many Americans have been willing to tolerate a burgeoning death toll.

In addition to compassion fade, a psychological state that sets in when the number of deaths reaches the point that the victims are viewed as mere statistics as opposed to individuals, studies have shown that the deaths of some people bother us more than others. The Moral Machine Game, developed by researchers at the Massachusetts Institute of Technology in 2018, is aimed at assessing how people engage in ethical decision-making around which groups of people and non-human animals should be saved, as a means of informing advancements in automated technology. Participants from 233 countries and territories were presented with scenarios in which they were forced to decide whether to change the course of an out-of-control driverless car, evaluating the consequences for passengers and a range of pedestrians, including babies, children, adults, pregnant women, the elderly, doctors and other professionals, the obese, handicapped, homeless individuals, dogs, and cats.[4] The results of the Moral Machine

Game experiments highlight that America's willingness to accept the devastating number of deaths from COVID-19 cannot be separated from that fact that the elderly, the poor, and individuals of color have been those most likely to die from coronavirus and that the weight assigned to these lives reflects entrenched attitudes with respect to a hierarchy of human value. Doctors have been thrust into their own form of the Moral Machine Game from which there is no escape, and I argue that the moral injury arising from the choices they encounter around end-of-life decision-making for patients is enhanced by a cultural norm that continues to view death as a failure and, thus, distinctly un-American.

The battle over individual rights versus collective responsibility is once again taken up in "On Snowflakes, Chilly Climates, and Shouting to Be Heard: The Role of Liberal Education in Weathering Campus Storms." This essay details a series of cases illustrating the complexities of balancing freedom of expression, inclusion, and equity on college campuses in an age of social media and amid renewed calls for colleges and universities to countenance and address the roles they have played in perpetuating institutionalized racism and White supremacy.

In this ostensibly post-truth era, when speech containing mass distortions and "alternative facts" aimed at the suppression of dissenting speech rather than the invitation of further speech prevails, the foundational principle that "more speech is better" is being challenged on college campuses by those who note that the burdens of unfettered speech are not borne equally. These challenges, similar to the charges made by Governor Whitmer against President Trump, have been met by accusations of a liberal bias, resulting in a flurry of legislation at both the state and federal levels containing threats to remove funding from colleges and universities that fail to safeguard free expression.

The concomitant introduction of legislative orders that prohibit certain speech related to antibias training, anti-Israeli sentiment, and curricula such as the 1619 Project, which is viewed as unpatriotic, have resulted in confusion over how college leaders should respond to conflicting orders. While many of these federal orders were vacated upon the election of President Biden, several state legislatures have taken up where President Trump left off. Deeper concerns have been raised with respect to the ways in which weaponizing speech in service to a partisan agenda has threatened to undermine the fundamental assumptions that good ideas triumph in the marketplace of ideas and that free speech inevitably serves to strengthen democracy. In an effort to address these concerns, the chapter ends with a consideration of the unique role that liberal education plays in facilitating points of merger around the common good—including the ideals we strive for and the sacrifices we are willing to make—in a diverse, pluralistic society.

This leads to a fuller defense, in the third essay, of liberal education as essential to our nation's historic mission of educating for democracy, especially during times of extreme polarization and partisanship. The arguments offered in "Preparing Students for Work, Citizenship, and Life in the Twenty-First-Century: Reestablishing Liberal Education as a Public Good" take into account a growing economic and racial segregation in higher education and mounting pressure for students to engage in short-term, technical training that might lead to more immediate employability. However, despite an increasingly skeptical public, it posits liberal education as the best preparation for work, citizenship, and life in a future none of us can fully predict.

There is a renewed sense of urgency around the mandate of educating for democracy following the January 6, 2021, attack on the U.S. Capitol by armed insurrectionists seeking to prevent a vote certifying Joe Biden's Electoral College victory. Once again, charges of incitement to violence arose after President Trump's statement to his supporters, "If you don't fight like hell, you're not going to have a country anymore," coincided with thousands of protesters storming the seat of American democracy. Hundreds carried pro-Trump banners, Confederate flags, and signs that read "Stop the Steal," based on the lie that Joe Biden lost the election. Others brandished anti-Semitic symbols, including one man who wore a Camp Auschwitz T-shirt, signaling his support for the mass extermination of Jews. Five people, including one Capitol police officer, died that day, and more than 140 were injured.

Yet, the violence that erupted on January 6 went beyond the individual lives lost and bodily harm sustained. The insurrection constituted an attack on democracy itself. When the mob breached the Capitol Building, scrawling "Murder the Media" on the doors of the chambers, chanting "Hang Mike Pence," and eerily calling, "Nancy, where are you?" in an effort to find Nancy Pelosi and place her on trial, they assaulted democracy's most sacred values. Justice, liberty, and equality serve as the bedrock of our republic, and the right of Americans to self-determination is upheld by the peaceful transfer of power in the aftermath of free and fair elections. Subsequent hearings in the House and Senate on the Capitol police response to the insurgents drew further attention to inequities in how the officers dealt with the insurrectionists compared to the way in which the predominantly peaceful Black Lives Matter protesters were treated in Washington, D.C., the previous summer.

The events of January 6 call for an understanding of how we can move forward as a nation, restore trust in our society's institutions, and find hope in one another through our shared values and heritage. What connects the topics taken up in these chapters is their capacity to demonstrate how tumultuous current events test and reveal what we value and the ways in which a liberal education can help us to learn lessons from one another, while cultivating the personal and social responsibility necessary for furthering the common good.

The essays build upon comments delivered during the 2020 Malcolm Lester Phi Beta Kappa Lecture Series, hosted by Mercer University. They pay tribute to Dean Lester, former dean of the College of Arts and Sciences, by recognizing the critical role higher education, in general, and liberal education, in particular, play in preserving democracy and the extent to which, from our nation's inception, colleges and universities have continued to represent powerful institutional forces in catalyzing individual and societal transformation. Like the founders of Phi Beta Kappa, who in 1776 addressed the most pressing ethical, legal, and social issues of the day—slavery, a standing army in times of peace, the role of the commonwealth in promoting public virtue—Malcolm Lester, through his generosity in sponsoring the lecture series, has enjoined us to carry out the mission of the Society, to foster intellectual inquiry and freedom of thought, grounded in friendship and morality. I am deeply honored to participate in celebrating his life and legacy at Mercer University.

1

MORAL DISTRESS, MORAL INJURY, AND THE CONCEPT OF DEATH AS UN-AMERICAN

INTRODUCTION TO THE CONCEPT OF MORAL DISTRESS

In his exquisite essay on the significance of Albert Camus's 1947 novel *The Plague* in relation to the COVID-19 pandemic, philosopher Alain de Botton invites readers to reflect on the existential reality that "when it comes to dying, there is no progress in history, there is no escape from our frailty. Being alive always was and will remain an emergency."[1] De Botton reminds us that for Camus, the absurdity of suffering and random loss of life can be countered only through decency, striving to lessen the suffering of others. When Dr. Rieux, Camus's narrator, is asked to explain what he means by decency, the doctor simply replies, "Doing my job."[2]

For physicians, doing one's job entails a duty to treat, even during a life-threatening epidemic. As far back as 1847, the first Code of Ethics of the American Medical Association affirms this responsibility by stating, "When pestilence prevails, it is their duty to face the danger, and to continue their labors for the alleviation of the suffering, even at the jeopardy of their own lives."[3] This edict has persisted, and the most recent iteration of the code asserts that "individual physicians have an obligation to provide urgent medical care during disasters even in the face of greater than usual risks to physicians' own safety, health, or life."[4] Nevertheless, the guidance allows that providing care to individual patients should be evaluated against the ability to continue care into the future.

At the height of the pandemic, in considering how to balance professional and personal obligations, a cardiologist wrote a letter to the *New York Times* comparing the practice of sending doctors into hospitals with limited personal protective gear to asking firefighters in their street clothes to rescue people from a burning building on the verge of collapse. The difference, of course, is that for physicians there is the compounded risk of infecting their families due to exposure on the job. The stress of treating critically ill patients in unprecedented numbers has been multiplied by having to engage in isolation from their families, while confronting decisions over how to allocate the last ventilator or how much time to spend comforting a patient who is dying alone due to hospital-imposed bans on visitors, rather than tend to others who might be saved.

Just as the residents in Camus's fictional town of Oran, Americans have taken false comfort in the efficacies of modern science. But, as forklifts were loading body bags into freezer trucks that were mobilized outside of hospitals on the streets of New York to be used as makeshift morgues, the gravity of the situation in the United States became undeniable. The tragic suicide of Dr. Lorna Breen, director of the Emergency Department at New York Presbyterian Hospital, highlighted the toll this latest global healthcare crisis has taken on the mental health of hospital workers. Breen, who was on the front lines of treating COVID-19 patients in what was then the nation's hotspot, contracted the disease and was forced to return to her parents' Virginia home to recuperate. She described to them the horror of dealing with an onslaught of patients so monumental that some were dying in ambulances while waiting to be admitted.[5]

Breen's death provided a grim glimpse at the despair experienced by professional caregivers attending to COVID-19 patients—the scope of which is detailed in a study published in the *Journal of the American Medical Association*. The report chronicles a wave of depression, anxiety, insomnia, and psychological distress among 1,257 medical workers, with women and nurses experiencing particularly severe symptoms tied to the emotional labor of bolstering the well-being of others while suppressing their own.[6] Fear around the lack of personal protective equipment, being exposed to COVID-19 at work and then taking the infection home to family, not having access to rapid testing if symptoms appeared and subsequently propagating the infection at work, together with uncertainty over who would take care of their families and whether their institutions would support them if they became ill, were all factors cited by doctors, nurses, advance practice clinicians, and resident fellows during the first week of the pandemic.[7] In addition to the psychic trauma these healthcare providers experienced, they also noted significant moral distress.

My first encounter with the consequences of moral distress centered around a forty-year-old patient being treated for cancer of the palate who was brought to the emergency room suffering from delirium. He was subsequently admitted to the Intensive Care Unit (ICU) for treatment of an overdose. The patient, who had an extensive history of alcohol and drug abuse, was reporting cluster headaches and made very specific requests about the type of medication he wanted, along with the method of delivery—two injections, fifteen minutes apart, one in each buttock. The covering physician was not only concerned about what he identified as drug-seeking behavior but also about the effects of the requested medication on the patient's already precarious respiratory status. As a result, the doctor ordered a nurse on the floor to administer a placebo. After the nurse adamantly refused, the physician became belligerent.

When the case was brought to the ethics committee by the nursing supervisor, we talked not only about the ethics of giving placebos but also about the phenomenon of moral distress experienced by the nurse who was ordered to do something she believed was unethical. In fact, the term "moral distress" was coined in 1984 by philosopher Andy Jameton, within the context of nursing ethics, to refer to situations in which institutional and organizational cultures coerce individuals to act in ways that go against their ethical principles. Ethical dilemmas, by their very nature, are such that no matter what course of action one takes, some ethical principle or norm will be violated. It is the continual overriding of what one regards as the correct moral principles that leads to moral distress.

Since the identification of the experience of moral distress as a potential consequence of decision-making for nurses, there has been considerable research concerning its impact on both the professional and personal lives of individuals. Today, moral distress continues to be a common topic in the nursing literature, with one study indicating that as many as 80 percent of nurses experience medium to high levels of moral distress and that more than 15 percent of nurses have left their jobs because of it.[8] Increasingly, however, there is a recognition that nurses are not the only healthcare providers experiencing moral distress and that this condition is having an equally deleterious effect on a wide range of caregivers, including physicians.

Though doctors traditionally occupy a different position in hospital hierarchies than nurses, social workers, and other healthcare team members, they are at times no less constrained by the institutional forces that lead to the psychic fallout from a broad range of ethical confrontations. While the framework for resolving complex dilemmas in medical ethics and the principles upon which the deliberation is grounded—beneficence, autonomy derived from respect for persons, and justice—remain unchanged, the pivot to a public health model of ethics that was necessitated by the COVID-19 pandemic resulted in new levels of moral distress for practitioners trained in a culture that has privileged a patient-centered ethic.

Indeed, transitioning to a focus on the welfare of the community has, at times, led to treatment decisions at odds with what might be in the best interest of specific individual patients. As the pandemic unfolded, finite critical-care support, including staff, beds, and equipment, made it such that optimal patient care was not always feasible. Surge capacity—the ability of hospitals to provide medical care amid a rapid influx of patients—is a fundamental component of disaster preparedness, and adequate planning requires a consideration of the needs of ICU patients over time, factoring in resource constraints that are likely to manifest. However, even when implementing well-developed surge-response strategies, hospitals can become overwhelmed.

The rapid exhaustion of critical-care capacity as the pandemic took hold in the United States precipitated reverse triage, a utilitarian approach of providing intensive therapy to those with the greatest chance of benefiting, denying admission to those who are deemed capable of surviving without hospitalization, and offering comfort measures alone for those with the bleakest prognoses. A public health framework centered on the greatest good, or the least amount of harm, for the maximum number of people went directly counter to the training of most U.S. physicians, which emphasizes patient autonomy, preferences, and values. Moreover, for doctors unaccustomed to rationing care in a manner that prioritizes patients most likely to survive over the sickest, moral distress arose around feelings that they were abandoning their patients and not fulfilling their ethical obligations.

Beyond the profound challenges arising from the immediate crisis of a pandemic, burgeoning moral distress among physicians has become a feature of routine medical practice. To understand why, consider the daily dilemmas doctors face when advocating for hemodialysis treatment for an undocumented immigrant, knowing that hospital policies proscribe it, except in cases of emergency; responding to pressures as a member of a group family-practice to see growing numbers of patients for shorter periods of time under a system of Relative Value Units; conveying concerns to administrators about the volumes of electronic medical records that are now being produced and that one suspects may actually undermine rather than enhance patient safety; maintaining one's own professional autonomy while both negotiating with families, out of a genuine commitment to shared decision-making, and addressing the demands of risk managers; fighting with insurers over the lack of coverage for a treatment deemed in the patient's best interest; or deciding whether to order needed testing and treatment for patients with limited or no medical insurance.

Each of these circumstances can cause moral distress among physicians, and a public health crisis has emerged over the past few years in which moral distress among physicians has evolved into moral injury—a phenomenon that coincides with their currently having the highest suicide rate of any profession. With one doctor committing suicide in the United States every day, the number of physician suicides is more than twice that of the general population.[9] Physicians Wendy Dean and Simon Talbot were the first to apply the concept of moral injury in conversations around physician burnout that surpasses moral distress. They describe moral injury as a feeling of "mental, emotional, and spiritual distress" after "perpetrating, failing to prevent, or bearing witness to acts that transgress deeply held moral beliefs and expectations."[10]

A phrase that was initially applied to the suffering experienced by military veterans whose psychological injuries were incapable of being addressed through standard treatments for post-traumatic stress disorder, "moral injury" for physicians is a consequence of "the agony of being constantly locked in double binds when every choice one makes yields a compromised outcome and when each decision contravenes the reason for years of sacrifice."[11] Dean and Talbot cite the growing number of circumstances under which they were unable to keep the oath to put their patients first, arising when "the imperatives of business trump the imperative of healing."[12] The subsequent damage to the doctor's moral foundation is a function of the problems themselves being systemic. Because the solutions are social, economic, and political rather than medical, they require collective action that reaches beyond the doctor's office or hospital campus.

In my experience as an ethics committee member for community hospitals, teaching hospitals at major universities, biobanks, and state health departments, undoubtedly the most significant rise in instances of moral distress and moral injury among physicians relates to end-of-life issues. And this has certainly been borne out by the pandemic, as doctors were left to make decisions, in the absence of clear advance healthcare directives, about whether to discontinue life support or to engage in aggressive treatment of patients they were just meeting for the first time.

With COVID-19 patients, the swift escalation of intubation left little time for discussion, and conversations with family members took on added complexities given that they were often required to be done by phone or video conference, impacting the quality of the communication by obscuring nonverbal cues and creating psychological distance. Predictably, doctors treating patients whose families must make decisions on their behalf experience higher levels of moral distress if there has never been a conversation about what the patient would want. As COVID-19 spread, doctors began turning to the public to encourage end-of-life planning and to each other for support in understanding how best to facilitate these discussions under such dire circumstances.

Though ethical issues at the end of life are nothing new, Americans' deeply entrenched attitudes about death are a contributing factor both in the pervasiveness of the problem faced by physicians around end-of-life decision-making for coronavirus patients and in an apparent shift regarding the types of cases that are being brought forward on a regular basis. My objective is to provide an overview of some contemporary challenges in bioethics with respect to decisions around death and dying in the United States and discuss how physicians, bioethicists, and the public can work together to reform a fragile system that is being further eroded by current cultural forces.

A SHIFT IN THE NATURE OF ETHICAL DILEMMAS RELATED TO END-OF-LIFE DECISION-MAKING

I want to begin by contrasting two cases that represent what I regard as a radical transition in the nature of ethical dilemmas related to end-of-life decision-making. The first case was relayed to me during a visit to our family practitioner. While sitting on the examining table, clad in my paper gown, I waited as the doctor finished typing notes in my record. Without turning around, he said: "Let me ask you something. You are still on the ethics committee, aren't you? My partner has this case, and I'm wondering if the committee might help."

He went on to describe an eighty-eight-year-old poststroke victim who was hospitalized repeatedly for congestive heart failure, diabetes, recurring pneumonia, open wounds, and staph infections. Each hospitalization involved a three- to four-week stay. Throughout these stays, the patient was intermittently conscious and incompetent to make decisions for herself. Since she was unable to swallow, she was fed using peripheral intravenous lines. The patient's daughter, who would leave her mother's side only occasionally to sit in her car, insisted that everything be done to keep her mother alive. It was during the most recent hospitalization, when a mass was discovered in the patient's lung, that questions of futility arose. The daughter demanded that a biopsy be performed and wanted surgery if the mass turned out to be cancerous. The medical team was convinced that the patient should be allowed to die, yet the daughter was intent on doing everything possible to sustain her mother's life. "What's frustrating," my doctor confessed, "is that the staff feels like we are torturing this poor woman, but the last time we were able to have the next of kin declared incompetent to make medical decisions, the hospital lawyers insisted that we do everything to keep the patient alive anyway."

As I was listening, I kept thinking about what a profound departure this case presented from the types of end-of-life issues the ethics committee dealt with when I first began practicing medical ethics in the mid-1980s. Then, almost all the scenarios that evoked moral distress involved patients or their families insisting on the right to refuse life-sustaining treatment in order to "die a natural death with dignity." One of the most compelling cases, foregrounding the physician's self-described moral distress, was brought to us for retrospective analysis. It involved a sixty-year-old woman who had been in failing health over the previous two years. Diagnosed with multiple vague symptoms, a final panel of tests revealed terminal liver cancer. When her primary care physician met with her to discuss the diagnosis and prognosis, he found the patient understandably shaken, but seemingly accepting of her fate. She made plans for the eventuality of her death by signing a Living Will, expressing her wishes to have life-sustaining treatment withheld if the burdens of treatment were likely to outweigh the benefits. She also made clear that she did not want to be resuscitated if death were imminent and she suffered cardiac arrest.

A copy of the patient's advance directive was on file in her doctor's office and in the emergency room when she was brought in by ambulance the day after she met with her doctor. Her husband discovered the patient in bed, unconscious from swallowing a bottle of tranquilizers, and blood-soaked, after having cut her wrists with a butcher's knife. The family physician, who happened to be on call in the emergency room when his patient was brought in, was the one who brought the case to us. He had known this patient for years and was absolutely convinced that she would not want to be resuscitated. In fact, he was concerned that if she survived, she would seek to have him charged with battery for going against her wishes by trying to save her life. On the other hand, he was cognizant that if he failed to treat her aggressively, he could be charged with assisted suicide, which is a felony in the state in which this occurred. Nonetheless, he believed it might be in his patient's best interest if he did nothing, since she likely had no good days ahead of her. In the end, however, he knew that living wills were not binding in responding to acts of attempted suicide and took the steps necessary to try to save her life. He performed cardiopulmonary resuscitation when she went into cardiac arrest, had her intubated, and stitched her up.

As he suspected, when his patient regained consciousness, she was furious. She tried to rip out the tubes attached to her and demanded that all treatment be stopped. A psychiatric consult was brought in to assess the patient's competency, she was deemed competent to refuse treatment, was extubated, and died six hours later. Though at first convinced that he had ultimately done the right thing under the circumstances, the physician regretted his part in extending his patient's suffering. In this case, he thought prolonged existence might bring about more harm than would death.

Akin to the previous case, moral distress arose, but here it was due to the fact that the doctor believed in order to meet his obligation to his patient based on a professional duty to both nonmaleficence (to do no harm) and to beneficence (to relieve suffering), he would have to go against his own self-interest in violating a legal code. In weighing his self-interest against the interest of another, he was forced to come to grips, not only with his patient's humanity but with his own as well. It was perhaps acknowledging the commonality of experience that enabled the physician to engage in a consideration of this case from a variety of perspectives, including a feminist perspective, when we were discussing it in the ethics committee.

By doing so, he came to understand how imbalances of power that are based on gender play themselves out in medical practice and in the theory surrounding that practice. As a result, he became aware that the moral distress he experienced was, in part, due to the realization that his patient's right to refuse life-sustaining treatment as an expression of the right to autonomy needed to be considered in the broader context of a society in which women are conditioned to be caregivers and may be psychologically pressured into choosing death rather than risk being an economic or emotional burden on their family members. After the patient's death, the doctor wondered, in the long run, whether a law allowing for physician-assisted suicide would have given this woman the assurance she needed that she would not be forced to suffer needlessly if death were imminent—a kind of assurance that may have prevented her from ever having taken the steps to actively end her own life, with or without the assistance of another.

Side by side, these cases illustrate the type of revolutionary transformation that has emerged as ethics committees confront end-of-life issues brought forward by physicians. Despite the movement away from cases involving the right to refuse life-sustaining treatment toward those centering on futility, in both instances the moral distress results from a common source. We live in a society in which technological advancements have preceded thoughtful reflection regarding the ethical, legal, and social implications of the use of that technology with respect to when and how patients should be allowed to die.

In the future, we will not be able to continue to avoid the ethical and policy issues inextricably linked to the use of medical technology. Questions that policy makers need to address in an open discussion include: How should society allocate scarce medical resources? Can individualism be excessive in matters of life and death? How can we balance the values of pluralism and tolerance, on the one hand, against principles of fairness to all, on the other? And most importantly, should our society continue to view death as a failure and, thus, distinctly un-American?[13]

In order to meaningfully address these questions, we need to confront two current trends. The first is the tendency toward interpreting patients' autonomy rights as including the right to demand whatever treatment is necessary for sustained existence. The second is responding to such cases with a liability-driven ethic. It is important to note from the outset that these trends are not only interrelated; they also are rooted in and bolstered by a deep-seated proclivity in American society to want to avert death at all costs and to avoid any open discussion of death.

The reluctance of Americans to talk about death is evidenced by findings from a 2015 Kaiser Health Foundation survey indicating that while 89 percent of patients believed a discussion with their physician around end-of-life preferences was important, only 17 percent reported having one.[14] Even among cancer patients, most of whom want to be involved in decision-making around end-of-life care, fewer than 40 percent have advance care planning conversations.[15] And with a completion rate of only 10 percent, Blacks have 77 percent lower odds of completing an advance directive around end-of-life care than Whites, while Latinxs have a 70 percent lower chance.[16]

AN EROSION OF TRUST AND RACIAL DISPARITIES

Certainly, finances have been one factor in low completion rates for all individuals, and it wasn't until January 1, 2016, that a reimbursement mechanism became effective for end-of-life planning through explicit physician-patient conversations under Medicare. However, there are broader cultural and social factors at play that mitigate against progress in enhancing the number of such interactions. One primary factor is an eroding relationship of trust among patients and physicians. The growth in managed care, which has led to doctors spending less time with patients, high-profile cases surrounding medical malpractice, and public access to medical information through the Internet has fueled skepticism among patients and increased fears that physicians will fail to act in their best interest.

Trust in doctors' commitments to promoting patient welfare is lowest among Blacks—a perspective informed by legacies of racism and White supremacy that have pervaded all societal institutions, including medicine. Black patients are still less likely to have their symptoms taken seriously, resulting in lower triage scores than Whites for the same reported medical complaints. In addition, they have longer wait times in the emergency room, and once seen, spend shorter amounts of time than White patients with doctors. Black patients are also more likely than Whites to be viewed as being dishonest about their symptoms.[17] Because trust is a foundational element in therapeutic relationships, patient care is inevitably impacted by hidden biases and institutional practices, leading to a breakdown in confidence among Black patients.

These attitudes of mistrust and suspicion among members of the Black community have been reinforced by a phenomenon known as the "Tuskegee effect," arising from the government's infamous syphilis study, launched in 1932 by the U.S. Public Health Service. The study, involving six hundred Black men in Alabama, tracked the progress of the disease in human subjects who were deliberately left untreated without their consent. The program persisted through 1972, when it was exposed as violating human dignity and individual rights. Beyond the horrific impact on the men and their families, the study is also proven to have shaped Black cultural perspectives on physicians and the entire medical system by encouraging a belief in medical conspiracies and stoking fears of medical exploitation.[18]

A research study conducted by Marcella Alsan and Marianne Wanamaker, more than four decades after the experiments were halted, indicates the enduring impact of the "Tuskegee Study on Untreated Syphilis on the Negro Male." They note that by 1980, the revelation of the wrongdoing that precipitated the development of new guidelines for ethical treatment of human subjects under the Belmont Report coincided with a reduced life expectancy among Black men forty-five years of age and older—a reduction of up to 1.5 years.[19]

Alsan and Wanamaker conclude that the revelations about abuses in the Tuskegee study accelerated mistrust of the medical community among Blacks, consequently discouraging health-seeking behavior and healthcare utilization and leading to higher rates of mortality. Individuals who suffered the most serious effects were those who lived in the closest geographic proximity to Macon County, where the study took place. These Black men could readily imagine themselves in the same position as those experimented on.[20] The lesson learned is that when racism is a risk factor, patients, as in this case, may choose to forgo even necessary medical services.

Despite high levels of concern among Black individuals regarding the integrity of the medical profession, members of the Latinx community are the ones least likely to visit a doctor. In fact, more than one-fourth of Latinx adults in the United States are without a regular healthcare provider, and nearly half never encounter a medical professional within year. The causes range from the lack of health insurance and concern over undocumented status by immigrants to language barriers and discomfort with American healthcare traditions, which rely on prescription drugs over "natural remedies."[21]

Among Latinxs, trust is also a factor, with one study of Latinx women confirming that the amount of information they disclose to doctors depended on whether they have developed a trusting relationship founded on mutual respect. A willingness to share their medical histories and current symptoms decreased when Latinx women patients could not sense compassion in their caregivers. Discomfort with physicians was magnified when doctors asked about taboo subjects such as sexual health and practices or mental illness. The same reticence applies to talk about death. While these patients reported feeling more at ease with doctors who share their cultural background, there is a persistent and unfortunate dearth of Latinx physicians.[22]

Distrust of medical professionals is reinforced among communities of color when purportedly objective principles end up reflecting hidden biases and structural racism. During any health emergency, death and hospitalization rates tend to be higher for minoritized groups. Three months after the World Health Organization declared COVID-19 a pandemic, the Centers for Disease Control and Prevention in Atlanta confirmed that the hospitalization rates for Black, American Indian, and Alaska Native populations were the highest, at five times the rate of Whites, followed by Hispanics and Latinxs, who had a rate of hospitalization four times that of Whites.[23] Though both the *Journal of the American Medical Association* (*JAMA*) and the *New England Journal of Medicine* (*NEJM*) published guidelines for the ethical allocation of scarce medical resources that affirmed the consensus that the nature and quality of healthcare should never be dependent upon the race, sex, religion, intellectual disability, insurance status, wealth, citizenship, social status, or connections of patients, critics have raised concerns that the recommendations offered in these publications fail to take into account how institutionalized racism influences their implementation.[24]

One example of such hidden biases can be discerned from a consideration of the implications of adhering to the consequentialist principle of maximizing benefits, central to the ethical guidelines that are detailed. Under circumstances where there are insufficient resources to go around, public health policies prioritize doing the greatest good for the greatest number of patients. Removing a patient from a ventilator or ICU bed is deemed permissible to save those with a better prognosis, even without the patient's consent, and healthcare providers are enjoined to make patients aware of this possibility upon admission. Whether or not a patient receives a ventilator or an ICU bed in the first place is based on an 8-point scale, with lower scores reflecting a greater likelihood of benefiting from critical care. The criteria include the probability of surviving to hospital discharge, assessed in relation to the severity of acute illness, and the patient's chances of achieving long-term survival, measured by the presence of comorbid conditions. In addition, by subtracting points from their overall score, preference is given to those considered vital to the public health response. The *NEJM* also recommends prioritizing treatment intervention for patients who have "participated in research to prove the safety and effectiveness of vaccines and therapeutics." If there is a tie, priority is given to those who are younger and have had less of an opportunity to go through the stages of the human life cycle.[25]

Applying these standards will have a disparately negative impact on mortality rates for those who are already the most vulnerable and underserved members of society. Assigning value based on long-term chances of survival and the presence of underlying conditions systematically disadvantages African American, Hispanic, and American Indian patients, who, due to environmental racism among other factors, are much more likely than Whites to be immunocompromised and suffer from chronic lung disease, moderate to severe asthma, heart disease, obesity, diabetes, chronic kidney disease requiring dialysis, and liver disease. Furthermore, life expectancy is directly correlated to zip codes, with residents of predominantly Black Harlem having a life expectancy at birth of 72.7 years of age, whereas residents of the majority White Upper East Side, five miles away, have a life expectancy at birth of 89. Therefore, considerations of life expectancy when calculating who should receive treatment are also fraught with the potential for racial bias.[26]

The same is true when it comes to giving priority to those who have participated in research trials or are healthcare providers. For reasons already discussed, Blacks and Latinxs are woefully underrepresented in clinal trials, with a participation rate of 5 percent and 1 percent respectively.[27] Furthermore, given that White workers are overrepresented in twenty-three of the thirty medical occupations, an otherwise laudable basis for judgment becomes suspect with respect to claims that it is color-blind.[28]

Black and Latinx Americans are much less likely than Whites to have advance directives, meaning that they are at increased risk of there being a misalignment between the care that they receive and their preferences. This fact, together with the threat of hidden biases determining the outcomes for patients during times of public health crises in which scarce resources must be allocated, showcases the urgency of healthcare providers having advance care conversations with patients in their care.

However, patients are not always the ones in the doctor-patient relationship who are reluctant to talk about death. Forty-eight percent of healthcare providers say they have struggled with identifying the right time to approach their patients regarding end-of-life decision-making because they did not want those in their care to think that they were giving up on them. Forty-six percent were hesitant to approach their patients with these issues because these doctors did not want them to lose hope.[29] These findings reflect the reality that physicians sometimes privilege concerns about how their patients will react to such conversations above the genuine and sometimes urgent need to be direct and straightforward when discussing goals of treatment at the end of life.

This choice in prioritization can lead to unintended consequences, including emotional, psychological, and financial harm, as illustrated by a controversial California court case, *Arato v. Avedon,* regarding the nature of informed consent in treating a dying patient. Upon his death from pancreatic cancer, Miklos Arato's family sued both his surgeon and his oncologist for giving Mr. Arato too much hope by offering chemotherapy and radiation without outlining the statistical morbidity of those with his condition. Whereas the plaintiffs argued that an understanding of statistical life expectancy was an essential component of informed consent, the doctors emphasized that Arato appeared to have such anxiety about his condition that it would have been medically inappropriate to hammer home the unlikelihood of the treatment's success.[30]

The case hinged upon the legal duty of doctors to disclose all material information to their patients so that the patient can make an informed decision regarding the recommended treatment or care. Mr. Arato and his family were told that most victims of pancreatic cancer die from the disease, and if he were to have a recurrence after chemotherapy and radiation, the disease would be considered incurable.

However, the oncologist, Dr. Avedon, argued that in his experience, patients in Mr. Arato's circumstances "wanted to be told the truth, but did not want a cold shower."[31] He argued that it would be medically inadvisable to deprive a patient of all hope, which would be the likely result of full disclosure of the disease's high mortality rates. Besides, as each of the testifying physicians argued, the statistical data cannot accurately predict what will happen in any specific case. Still, studies indicate that a physician who is not direct can inadvertently mislead a patient about his or her prognosis and treatment goals.[32]

Arato v. Avedon makes abundantly clear that when a ruling of negligence comes down to the question of "How much hope is too much hope?," institutional vectors for engaging in values conversations become critically important. Medical ethicist Larry Churchill maintains that the medical profession's informal rule that a clinician should never take away a patient's hope—which often serves as a rationale for deception around a terminal diagnosis, offering experimental procedures with little promise and substantial risk, and failing to provide specifics in a diagnosis—reflects a misunderstanding around how hope works. He points out that part of the problem is the faulty assumption that physicians can predict what people hope for, which is not always survival. Instead, it may be reconciliation with a family member or ensuring the well-being of their loved ones when they are gone. Reminding us that "the most powerful forms of hope may not have a hoped-for object at all," Churchill contends that "hope does not gain its power by relying on probabilities. Although grounded in realism, it is an openness to being surprised by goodness or what theologically is often called 'grace.'"[33]

Churchill's sentiments echo those of physician Jerome Gruber, who in his book *The Anatomy of Hope* insists that "true hope has no room for delusion." Gruber admits that "For all my patients, hope, true hope, has proved as important as any medication I might prescribe or any procedure I might perform." Yet true hope, unlike false hope, carries courage and resilience that "is rooted in an unalloyed reality" and "is not initiated and sustained by completely erasing fear and anxiety."[34] The challenge, of course, is fostering true hope within a death-denying culture.

THE POLITICS OF DEATH

Throughout the past decade, the rhetoric surrounding various proposals for healthcare reform highlights just how uncomfortable Americans on both sides of the doctor-patient relationship are when talking about death. In a society in which television viewers are barraged with invitations to ask their physicians about drugs that will extend the life of those with small cell lung cancer and treatment for erectile dysfunction, nicotine addiction, bipolar depression, A-fib, arthritis or fibromyalgia pain, the side-effects of chemotherapy, diabetes, eczema and psoriasis, Chronic Obstructive Pulmonary Disease, Crohn's disease, and a host of other maladies, there was a staggering amount of Sturm und Drang during the drafting of the Patient Protection and Affordable Care Act over the proposed inclusion of a provision that would reimburse physicians for talking to their patients about advance directives for end-of-life decisions or hospice care. Rumors of death panels and invocations of Nazi euthanasia programs led politicians to excise the proposal early on from the House Tri-Committee bill.

The furor started with a post on Sarah Palin's Facebook page asserting that if the government passed healthcare legislation, boards would be set up to determine whether the elderly and disabled were worthy of care. On August 7, 2009, she wrote:

> As more Americans delve into the disturbing details of the nationalized health care plan that the current administration is rushing through Congress, our collective jaw is dropping, and we're saying not just no, but hell no!
>
> The Democrats promise that a government health care system will reduce the cost of health care, but as the economist Thomas Sowell

has pointed out, government health care will not reduce the cost; it will simply refuse to pay the cost. And who will suffer the most when they ration care? The sick, the elderly, and the disabled, of course. The America I know and love is not one in which my parents and my baby with Down Syndrome will have to stand in front of Obama's "death panel" so his bureaucrats can decide, based on a subjective judgment of their "level of productivity in society," whether they are worthy of healthcare. Such a system is downright evil.[35]

Though garnering the most attention, Palin was not the first to raise these types of concerns. Her post followed an earlier editorial in the *Washington Times* on how government plans for more funding for health information technology could be compared to Nazi eugenics programs.[36] In addition, on a program hosted by the actor, Republican senator, and then conservative radio talk-show host Fred Thompson, the former lieutenant governor of New York, Betsy McCaughey, commented that "Congress would make it mandatory—absolutely require—that every five years people in Medicare have a required counseling session that will tell them how to end their li[ves]sooner."[37] She misstated, perhaps out of genuine confusion, the real intent of the legislation, which was to have Medicare pay for optional appointments to discuss living wills, healthcare directives, and other end-of-life issues.

In the weeks that followed, there were statements issued by politicians warning against a policy that would push us toward "government-encouraged euthanasia" and stressing the need to protect seniors from "being put to death by their government."[38] President Obama responded by maintaining: "Some of people's concerns have grown out of bogus claims spread by those whose only agenda is to kill reform at any cost. The best example is the claim, made not just by radio and cable talk show hosts, but prominent politicians, that we plan to set up panels of bureaucrats with the power to kill off senior citizens. Such a charge would be laughable if it weren't so cynical and irresponsible."[39] Misinformation and fake news around death panels did indeed take a toll on progress toward healthcare reform. Yet, by disavowing the truth of the claim of death panels in this way, President Obama failed to address the fear underlying the concerns of those who readily believed the rhetoric, namely the denial of necessary medical care at a time of urgent need. Thus, an opportunity was lost for meaningful debate over critical end-of-life issues that were pushed aside during the process of political jockeying.

People are afraid that the government will be allowed to determine what constitutes necessary care and who should be allowed to receive it. Americans want such decisions to be made by families in consultation with their doctors. Nevertheless, they may not fully comprehend the extent to which the current norms, which discourage conversations around end-of-life issues and rely on the myth that we do not already have a system of healthcare rationing, serve to thwart their ultimate desires. My goal here is not to dredge up partisan debates but instead to draw attention to the ways in which, when it comes to policies and practices in matters of life and death, the burdens and benefits of the current healthcare system are not borne equally.

Nowhere is this more evident than with the COVID-19 crisis. Ironically, some of the same politicians and commentators who were fueling outrage over fictional death panels a decade ago issued clarion calls for states to reopen, get the economy moving, and "let the elderly take a chance on . . . survival in exchange for keeping the America that all America loves for your children and grandchildren."⁴⁰ What was left out of this rhetoric was an acknowledgment of the disparately negative impact of COVID-19 on communities of color due to persistent structural inequities in healthcare, income, wealth, education, access to government resources, and incarceration.

At a time when America was experiencing a dramatic surge in the number of coronavirus cases, the outcome of this strategy was the emergence of the real equivalent of death panels resulting from the implementation of crisis standards of care in response to inadequate supplies of ventilators, blood, beds, doctors, and nurses. Accompanied by delays in routine surgery, in the screening for and treatment of cancer, heart disease and other life-threatening conditions, alongside the elimination of face-to-face doctors' visits for patients with chronic illnesses, decision-making about who should be prioritized in receiving a hospital bed deepened existing racial inequalities in healthcare.

HOW WE DIE AND
THE BEST CARE POSSIBLE

Americans' inabilities to confront our inadequacies around death should not come as too much of a surprise to those familiar with the medical literature. In the mid-1990s, the *Journal of the American Medical Association* published a series of research papers resulting from a ten-year, multimillion-dollar study on how we die in America. Sponsored by the Robert Wood Johnson Foundation, the Study to Understand Prognoses and Preferences for Outcomes and Risks of Treatment (SUPPORT) was the largest, most widely publicized research project examining end-of-life care.[41] SUPPORT was comprised of a two-year observational study of 9,105 adult patients hospitalized with one or more of nine life-threatening diagnoses and an overall six-month mortality rate of 47 percent. The study took place in five teaching hospitals across the United States, with the objective of improving end-of-life decision-making and reducing the frequency of mechanically supported, painful, and prolonged dying processes.

Phase 1 of the study began with the observation of 4,301 patients, followed by a controlled clinical trial in the second year. In phase 2 of the trial, 4,804 patients and their physicians were randomized by specialty group and assigned to either the intervention group (n = 2,652) or the control group (n = 2,152). Physicians in the intervention group received daily updates for up to six months regarding the likelihood of the patient's survival over the six-month time-period, outcomes of CPR, and functional disability at two months. In addition, a specifically trained nurse was assigned to have multiple contacts with the patient, the patient's family, the physician, and hospital staff to identify preferences, improve an understanding of outcomes, heighten attention to pain control, and facilitate advance care planning and patient-physician communication.[42]

The phase 1 observation documented significant shortcomings in communication and the overuse of aggressive treatment, both at odds with the patient's wishes and characteristic of death in a hospital. Only 47 percent of physicians knew when their patients wanted to forgo CPR, and 46 percent of do-not-resuscitate (DNR) orders were written within two days of the patient's death. Among the patients who died, 38 percent spent at least ten days in an intensive care unit, and over 50 percent of conscious patients who died in the hospital reported to family members that they were in moderate to severe pain at least half the time, with the extension of life not correlated with an improved quality of life.[43]

During the phase 2 intervention, there was no demonstrable improvement in patient-physician communication, with only 37 percent of control patients and 40 percent of intervention patients discussing CPR preferences. The same lack of improvement was true with respect to the five targeted outcomes around the incidence and timing of written do-not-resuscitate orders; physicians' knowledge of patients' DNR preferences; the number of days spent in the ICU; receiving mechanical ventilation and what to do if comatose before death; and the level of reported pain. Furthermore, intervention failed to reduce the use of hospital resources in end-of-life care.[44]

The SUPPORT study revealed that dying in America had been unnecessarily painful, isolating, and costly, resulting from physicians either not understanding or ignoring their patients' wishes. While the study was designed to improve end-of-life decision-making and lessen suffering, the findings illustrated that none of the interventions introduced significantly influenced any of the outcomes. The researchers concluded that enhancing opportunities for greater patient-physician communication, which was advocated as the primary method for improving patient outcomes, may be inadequate for changing established practices. They called instead for a greater individual and societal commitment to address the issues, alongside more proactive and forceful measures within the medical community.[45]

The results of the SUPPORT study were so shocking to the funding agency that Robert Wood Johnson commissioned a series of papers done by the Hastings Center to explore the study's conclusions as to the circumstances in which many of us die and how difficult it may be to make that process any better. In the end, the funding agency reported, "One of the most insightful explanations of the SUPPORT results pointed to a popular and medical culture that so forcefully resists the notion of death that the families, health care practitioners, and patients themselves are unwilling to ask questions and make the kinds of decisions that would diminish the fear surrounding the process of dying in this country."[46]

To illustrate this point, in his article entitled "How We Lie," Boston University ethicist George Annas recounts surgeon Sherwin Nuland's experience with a patient, Hazel Welch, described in his best-selling book *How We Die*.[47] Welch was a ninety-two-year-old arthritis victim who suffered a perforated digestive tract after a fall. Though competent and adamant in her refusal of treatment, Nuland persists in his attempts to persuade his longtime patient to undergo surgery. Welch agrees reluctantly because she trusts her doctor. The operation is more complicated than expected, the suffering is intense afterward, and the patient dies from a stroke two weeks later. While Nuland at first says that he would have done things differently after this experience, he recants upon reflection. "It is a lie," he admits, for surgeons do everything, no matter what the cost to the patient, rather than risk the scorn of their peers.

Nuland remarks:

It is in such matters that ethicists and moralists run aground when they try to judge the actions of the bedside doctors, because they cannot see the trenches from their own distant viewing point. The code of the profession of surgery demands that no patient as salvageable as Miss Welch be allowed to die if a straightforward operation can save her, and we who would break the fundamental rule, no matter the humaneness of our motive, do so at our own peril. Viewed by a surgeon, mine was a strictly clinical decision, and ethics should not have been a consideration.[48]

Annas emphasizes that physicians are taught to do everything, and if there is nothing else that can be done, then to not talk about death. He is convinced that under these circumstances, the only way for there to be a change in the quality of dying is to take individuals out of hospitals before they die, or to never admit them in the first place. If a competent patient, clearly expressing her wishes, is not listened to, what chance do we have of being listened to when we are no longer competent? Annas suggests that our attitudes about death and dying are too deeply ingrained to be able to make a difference.

A quarter of a century after the release of the SUPPORT study, little has changed. A 2014 Institute of Medicine report, *Dying in America: Improving Quality and Honoring Individual Preferences near End of Life,* details the medical community's continuing inadequacies in addressing the goals of care, noting that more than one-fourth of Medicare dollars were spent on patients during the last year of life and that treatment was, at times, both ineffective and unwanted. The fact is that Americans are still reluctant to talk and think about death. For this reason, the process of dying, particularly in the hospital setting, is often characterized by feelings of abandonment and loss of control on the part of patients and their families. While more than two-thirds of people say they want to die at home, less than one-third do, and anticipation of a hospital death is often overwhelmed by fear that dying will involve a complex strategy designed solely to maintain vital functions rather than address human suffering and dignity. This fear is not unwarranted given that, more than ever, death has become a negotiated process rather than a discrete event. In the absence of meaningful collaboration, patients may be subject to overtesting, overtreatment, and rehospitalization at the expense of quality of life during one's last days.

A vast majority of Americans who die in healthcare institutions do so following a decision between the physician, patient, and family to forgo treatment. According to psychiatrist Lewis Cohen in his book *No Good Deed: A Story of Medicine, Murder Accusations, and the Debate over How We Die,* "fully 85 percent–or approximately 2 million–of the 2.4 million deaths occurring annually in the United States medical system are preceded by a structured decision to limit life-sustaining treatment."[49] He underscores the fact that "even in America's intensive care units–our country's most medically aggressive settings–more than three-quarters of an estimated 400,000 deaths are now preceded by treatment limitation decisions."[50] As a consequence, bioethicist Nancy Dubler maintains, "collaboration and negotiation will need to replace the raw exercise of power that appealing to 'futility' represents"–exercises that, in and of themselves, will require more meaningful conversations between families and healthcare providers around death.[51]

There has been a movement on the part of states to facilitate such efforts and take up where the federal government left off a decade ago in terms of promoting conversations around the best care possible at the end of life. In 2014, the Massachusetts Senate passed a bill to promote palliative care awareness, requiring "each licensed hospital, skilled nursing facility, health center or assisted living facility to distribute to patients in its care information regarding the availability of palliative care and end-of-life options."[52] This counseling includes the prognosis, risks, and benefits of various treatment options, and a detailing of the right to comprehensive pain and symptom management at the end of life. The mandate is to offer the information. Patients still have the right to decline a conversation and refuse the offer of making end-of-life plans. Nevertheless, the encouragement of such open conversations will assist healthcare teams in aligning the delivery of healthcare with the patient's wishes.

The Massachusetts law followed similar legislation in Michigan, California, and New York. The Michigan Dignified Death Act requires physicians to inform their patients with "reduced life expectancies" of the recommended medical treatment and alternatives, along with the risks, benefits, advantages, and disadvantages of each option. Patients are also informed about their ability to appoint someone to make healthcare decisions for them if they become unable to do so; their ability to receive, discontinue, or refuse treatment; and their ability to choose palliative care treatment and pain and symptom management.[53] California's Right to Know End-of-Life Options Act requires that healthcare providers make counseling available to terminally ill patients upon their request.[54] Under New York's Palliative Care Information Act, the first in the country, healthcare providers must offer to provide the counseling upon a terminal diagnosis.[55]

In each case, this legislation is premised on the notion that conversations around end-of-life care should not be initiated at a time when patients are at their most vulnerable, physically and emotionally. Instead, they should take place as a part of initial, routine, and ongoing visits to physicians. Authentic decisions—ones reflecting the deeply held values that patients have demonstrated throughout their lives—are enhanced by evolving conversations as the burdens of illness and benefits of treatment are continually assessed.

Legislation provides a pivotal starting point, and we should utilize as many strategies as possible to encourage physicians to discuss the goals of any specific treatment within the entire span of a patient's medical history. But there is no doubt that having integrated conversations regarding end-of-life issues as both a way of life and the standard of care is the most desirable approach, given that legal mandates often do little to change the culture that has served as the basis for reliance on the coercive power of the law in the first place. In addition, doctors often remain unaware of such laws, which are rarely enforced.

This points to the need for the development of competencies among medical staff that are better aligned with contemporary challenges in healthcare. Surgeon Atul Gawande, author of *Being Mortal: Medicine and What Matters in the End,* argues that "Scientific advances have turned the process of aging and dying into medical experiences. And we in the medical world have proved alarmingly unprepared for it."[56] Recounting the story of a patient facing paralysis who made clear, much to the surprise of his family, that for him, life is worth living as long as he can eat ice cream and watch football, Gawande insists that we must begin asking patients, "What are you fighting for? What are your priorities?"

Promoting these types of conversations was the catalyst behind the Conversation Project, launched in 2010. In collaboration with the Institute for Healthcare Improvement, the founders of the project, including columnist Ellen Goodman, are attempting to "spark cultural change at the kitchen table—not in the intensive care unit,"[57] so that it will become easier for people to communicate end-of-life wishes, expressed in advance and respected at the end. Two years after the inception of the project, the founders began exploring what it would mean for healthcare systems to be conversation-ready, ensuring that end-of-life care accords with what matters most to patients and respects their goals, preferences, and values. The researchers concluded that if they are to achieve sustainable reform, making health organizations conversation-ready requires transformation at both the system level and the individual patient-professional level.

In the past, major changes around the medical culture and patient advocacy have occurred at the system level when individuals have come together to call for reforms. Yet, as palliative care physician Ira Byock jokes in his book *The Best Care Possible,* "Being mortal is too broad a category to generate a special interest group."[58] Instead, physicians need to rally as a professional community to ensure adequate mentoring around stopping life-prolonging treatment, encouraging people to fill out advance directives, and improving pain management, while lobbying for end-of-life discussions as a routine component of medical practice. According to bioethicist Rebecca Dresser, "too many clinicians lack the skill, opportunity, or will to have the difficult conversations when patients and families cope with serious illness[,] . . . leaving patients and families to struggle largely on their own."[59] Therefore, this training needs to be incorporated into medical school curricula.

The persistent underreferral and underutilization of hospice care reflects a system of medical education in which most schools do not require hospice or palliative care rotations. In fact, the Liaison Committee on Medical Education that accredits medical schools currently does not require clinical rotations or courses on palliative medicine and end-of-life care. As a result, in 2016, 88 percent of medical residents reported little or no training around end-of-life care during their residencies.[60] This is true despite hospice care correlating with a higher quality of life for patients and easier bereavement processes for families. Findings of improved outcomes for patients in hospice care have led to recent proposals that call upon doctors to begin having conversations about hospice when it is estimated that the patient has a year to live—six months before the patient is eligible for admission to the program.

However, one barrier to this approach has been the Medicare Hospice Benefit law, passed in 1982, which requires patients to forgo curative care once they enter hospice. The forced choice between palliative care and curative care has contributed to fewer than half of eligible Medicare beneficiaries taking advantage of hospice services. Moreover, the average length of stay, twenty-four days, falls far short of recommendations for how much time patients should have under hospice care if their needs at the end of life are to be fully met.[61]

Recognizing the unintended consequences of the Medicare Hospice Benefit law, in 2016 the federal government began a five-year experiment to counter the obstacles it presented by working with hospices in forty states to offer end-of-life care and counseling at the same time. Under the Medicare Care Choices Model, patients can receive treatment to extend their lives alongside palliative care and counseling rather than having to choose one or the other. The hope with this reform is that in addition to improved healthcare services and quality of life for patients, hospital and home care staff will receive more comprehensive training in complying with patients' wishes. If this change in standards of care occurs, discussions of medical futility and palliative care, when necessary, will be less stressful for both parties in the physician-patient relationship.[62]

Beyond doctor-patient interactions, however, training around end-of-life conversations must extend to interactions among physicians. This is particularly true with the advent of hospitalists. Hospitalists emerged in the 1990s, reflecting a new model for acute inpatient care. Because they are based in hospitals, without the demands of a separate medical practice, the notion is that hospitalists will be better able to coordinate care for hospitalized patients in a manner that both controls costs and better serves the needs of individual patients. Since their introduction onto hospital healthcare teams, much research has supported the use of hospitalists as a means of offering the best care possible at the end of life. By the nature of their work, they offer enhanced accessibility, familiarity with hospital policies and procedures, and extensive experience in addressing the physical and psychological needs of hospitalized patients.[63]

Be that as it may, the pervasive use of hospitalists has added a layer of complexity around end-of-life negotiations. As primary care physicians spend less time in hospitals doing rounds with their patients, the most immediate challenge is that, as the attending of record, hospitalists often are required to make treatment decisions in consultation with patients and families they have just met. It can be difficult to meaningfully engage in a values inventory to inform treatment decisions with a patient who is sick enough to be hospitalized and with whom one has no prior history.

The single most significant determinant of the choices made by patients regarding end-of-life care is how their doctors communicate with them. A series of studies reveals that critically ill patients are more likely to select comfort-care measures if that was the default option they were randomly assigned by their physician in clinical trials. On the other hand, patients who were randomly assigned the default option of chest compressions, breathing machines, and feeding tubes were more likely to select these invasive measures.[64] Physicians need to know their patients well enough to guide decision-making that is most consistent with the patient's wishes. At the same time, they need to understand that when patients are left unguided, they are likely to follow what they believe the doctor wants them to do. Indeed, offering options to patients in the absence of guidance may unintentionally undermine the autonomy physicians are seeking to protect. For this reason, not offering a professional recommendation along with a prognosis is considered by many clinicians to be a failure in professional duties to patients. Concerns over paternalism can be alleviated by making an explicit recommendation that the patient understands can be rejected without having any bearing on the quality of care.

Moreover, medical students need to be taught not only how to discuss end-of-life issues with their patients but with one another as well. With hospitalists, the addition of another specialist onto the healthcare team increases the potential for ethical conflict. Oncologists and other specialists, hospitalists, palliative, and primary care physicians may have different perspectives regarding the aims and purposes of treatment. If the oncologist is recommending treatment that the hospitalist believes is futile, there may be a reluctance on the part of the hospitalist to challenge the oncologist by promoting a comfort-care-only strategy. The goals of medicine consist of healing, sustaining life, preserving functions, and alleviating suffering. Sometimes these are in conflict, and professional commitments based on the goals of medicine must guide behavior and serve as a model for adjudicating cases in ways that ultimately promote the best interest of the patient.

Therefore, in end-of-life situations requiring collaborative decision-making between a patient and healthcare team, values conversations involving all stakeholders are essential for protecting patients' rights.

Medical schools, especially in the wake of the coronavirus pandemic, have begun to respond to the need to bridge the gap between patients' wishes at the end of life and the care they receive. Recognizing that physicians' primary duties extend to facilitating discussions around death and dying, these conversations are being positioned as a necessary medical tool, as opposed to a burden. For this reason, medical educators are creating rotations within hospices, nursing homes, and assisted-living facilities with the goal of providing students and residents practice with the necessary communication, medical, and interpersonal skills for these types of interactions.

For instance, the new curriculum at the Tufts University School of Medicine includes a "Patient Experiences Thread" that spans all four years of medical school, focusing on end-of-life and palliative care, the impact of health on patients and their families, and advanced communication skills. Similarly, the Larner College of Medicine at the University of Vermont has adopted an integrative approach to training physicians around palliative and end-of-life care that incorporates an intensive third-year program aimed at enhancing pain management and empathy skills, identifying communication tools such as Vital Talk and the Serious Illness Care Program, and building resilience. At both institutions, medical students learn to listen critically and with understanding and to ask questions that will help them discern the patient's values. They participate in and observe others engaging patients in crucial conversations that encourage family members to tell stories about their loved ones, while helping patients to share their worries and concerns.[65]

However, if this improved, more comprehensive medical training is ever to have an impact on patient outcomes at the end of life, system-level changes must include changes in institutional structures and policies that support physicians by recognizing and allowing the time necessary to engage in these discussions. Setting up a patient-care conference with the relevant decision makers; reviewing the diagnosis, prognosis, and treatment options; creating the right tone for discussion; attending to the feelings of those involved; taking a values inventory; talking about Medical Orders for Life Sustaining Treatment (MOLST), living wills, and a durable power of attorney; constructing a plan for follow-up conversations; and building consensus among various constituencies are all extremely time-intensive. Yet, the century-old system of paying doctors based on volume rather than value has led to a reduction in the time necessary for having in-depth conversations around end-of-life wishes with each patient. It has also increasingly resulted in overtesting and overtreatment with little benefit in many instances.

Journalist Joe Klein broadcasts this feature of contemporary medical practice in a cover story for *Time Magazine,* in which he reports on his five-month experience as a participant in the type of collaboration and negotiation needed around end-of-life care for both his mother and his father, who were each suffering from dementia. He says, in the end: "My parents died serenely, with dignity. When you are a death panel—when the time and manner of their passing is at least partly in your hands—that is the very best you can hope for."[66] Klein believes that the difference in the quality of the dying experience for his parents was the result of his decision to transfer them from regular fee-for-service Medicare to a private nursing home that used the Geisinger heathcare system, in which physicians are paid salaries and outcomes-based performance bonuses rather than by the services they perform.

But the fact is that very few patients are afforded this option, or even the choice of doctors handling their end-of-life care. A friend of mine who is a pulmonologist tells me that for over 95 percent of the patients referred to him with end-stage lung disease, he is the first to bring up issues of end-of-life care. Still, by spending the time to discuss their hopes and fears, he is willing to risk being scolded by some administrator down the line because he lives by the principles underlying Francis Peabody's message to students at Harvard in his 1925 address on "The Care of the Patient" that "the secret of the care of the patient is in caring for the patient."[67] Nonetheless, fewer than 10 percent of practicing physicians support eliminating fee-for-service models, seeing "more as better—even when the scientific literature contradicts that perception."[68]

Finally, within the practice of medicine, all healthcare providers must be educated not only around cultural humility but about the impact of structural racism and the ways in which implicit biases lead to differential treatment at the end of life. Racism in American society, including in our healthcare system, has been declared a public health emergency,[69] and addressing this crisis mandates a review of policies and practices, along with a push toward diversifying the profession. Studies have shown that health and safety outcomes for patients are improved when patients receive care from practitioners who share their racial identity. Yet, only about 2.6 percent of the nation's doctors in 2019 and 7.3 percent of students enrolled in medical school in 2020 identified as Black or African American. In the same year, 2019, only 3.8 percent of doctors identified as Hispanic, Latinx, or of Spanish origin.[70] In order to make medical schools more equitable, their administrators must strive to have greater diversity among the faculty and staff and interrogate the ways in which their practices reproduce existing structures that marginalize Black and Latinx applicants.

Black and Latinx candidates are three times more likely than Whites to come from families with a combined income of less than $50,000. Yet, overall, the majority of medical school students come from upper- and middle-class families. In addition, selection committees have been shown to undervalue the academic experience of students who attended community colleges, even though those students are more likely to practice family medicine and serve the public health needs of underserved communities. Within medical schools, great strides in furthering diversity goals have been made when admission departments have adopted holistic admission processes that encompass a consideration of student experience, personal attributes, ability to respond to adversity, and academic history and when admitted students are provided with intensive mentoring and advising.[71]

Beyond what takes place in medical schools and in the corridors of hospitals, hospices, and nursing homes, efforts to transform cultural norms around death and dying must extend into communities themselves if they are ever to take hold. This is where bioethicists can play a critical role by serving as public intellectuals and conducting workshops with community members around end-of-life decision-making. The range and scope of work includes facilitating changes in the way we talk about death, replacing phrases such as "Do Not Resuscitate" with "Allow Natural Death," and "Full Code" with "Artificial Death Extension." These simple shifts in the language that is used can help allay people's fears that they will be forced to die if they have an advance directive indicating something other than "do everything possible to prolong life."

It also includes helping the public understand the intricacies of current legislation around end-of-life care. For example, in addition to the growing number of states with legislation that limits doctors' rights to deny life-sustaining treatment without consent, even when based on judgments of medical futility, forty-one states and the federal government have passed right-to-try legislation. Introduced at the state level in 2014, the intent of these laws is to enable access to experimental therapies not approved by the Food and Drug Administration (FDA) for terminally ill individuals. In 2018, President Trump signed Senate Bill 204 into law, targeting the Food and Drug Administration as the primary impediment to the dying gaining access to unapproved drugs.[72] But, because these drugs are the property of drug companies and their investors, not the FDA, there is no obligation on the part of drug manufacturers to provide the treatment. Further, there is no obligation for insurers to pay for the medication or for the doctors to prescribe the treatment in the first place. Indeed, despite President Trump's prediction that "thousands of lives would be saved," only a few patients have been able to benefit from the law, leading to its being framed by critics as "placebo legislation" that makes people feel better, without having any real impact.

As it stands, the FDA has for decades offered an expanded access or compassionate use program in which patients can request investigational drugs, even when they are not participating in a clinical trial. Though right-to-try proponents complained about the burdens imposed under the current system, the form that physicians must submit to the FDA for review after a drug company agrees to supply a patient with an experimental drug requires less than one hour to complete, and the FDA approves more than 99 percent of the requests. The mean turnaround time is between eight and twenty-six days, with emergency requests taking a day or less to be fulfilled. Nevertheless, there are further steps that can be taken to enhance the education of doctors and patients around expanded access and how drug companies can be encouraged to participate.[73] In the meantime, shifting the focus to what has turned out to be empty legislation will only harm patients and their families.

CHANGING ATTITUDES

At the grassroots level, there is cause for optimism in changing the cultural attitudes around death that have contributed to patient suffering at the end of life. Amid the greatest pandemic in more than century, there is a renewed opportunity for cultural transformation arising from a generational shift in attitudes around preparing for death. COVID-19 has affected the way many people are thinking about illness and end-of-life planning, signaled by twenty- and thirty-somethings flocking to a variety of emerging end-of-life start-ups designed help clients navigate their final wishes.

With the majority of new users under forty, companies such as Cake, Near, Lantern, A Gentler Parting, and Going With Grace have seen dramatic increases in traffic and have begun to share their resources on a Slack channel called "Death & Co." Some of these businesses have been founded with the goal of addressing the complexities of this moment of racial reckoning in America's history, when mourning over losses due to the coronavirus intersects with grief over acts of anti-Black racism. By directly confronting the challenge of how to have a good death in the absence of a good society, emerging Black-owned businesses are aimed at providing services to communities that acknowledge African American traditions of mourning, while encouraging end-of-life planning within a safe space. From death doulas and art, sound, music, and massage therapists to end-of-life photographers and videographers, a panoply of companies is being formed to offer a new brand of death-and-dying services.[74] There are professionals to help clients write wills, downsize their homes, place pets who will be left behind, create legacy projects, and provide grief management.

Millennials are also turning to social media to work through their anxieties about death and to cope with grief during the pandemic. These new venues are being utilized not just by individuals but by healthcare systems attempting to create institutional infrastructures and organizational cultures for promoting such conversations. In Massachusetts, for example, Partners HealthCare, Brigham and Women's Hospital, and Ariadne Labs, operated by the Harvard School of Public Health, have called upon Cake to distribute their end-of-life conversation guides and to solicit feedback on their resources. Providence Health Systems, a network of fifty-one hospitals and one thousand clinics in seven states, has also teamed up with Cake to encourage the use of its "trusted-decision-maker" form detailing end-of-life preferences.[75]

The trusted-decision-maker form is simple and straightforward. There are only two steps, and these can be completed online or on a printed sheet. The first step is to designate one or two trusted decision makers in the event that the dying person is incompetent or incapacitated. The second step is to choose one of the following options:

- I am not sure at this time which statements below I most agree with. I trust my trusted decision maker to do what is best for me.
- I want to continue living even if my quality of life seems low to others and I am unable to communicate with people. In general, I would accept support of my breathing, heart, and kidney function by machines that require me to be in a hospital or special care unit.
- Life is precious, but I understand that we all die sometime. I want to live as long as I can interact with others and can enjoy some quality of life. I would accept intensive treatments only if I had a reasonable chance of getting better. I would refuse long-term support by intensive medications or machines if my quality of life was poor and I was not able to communicate with people.
- It is most important to me to avoid suffering. I do not want extraordinary medical treatments, such as breathing machines or cardiopulmonary resuscitation (CPR). If my natural body functions fail, I would refuse treatments and choose to die naturally.

Because the form is not a legal document and does not require witnesses or the signature of a notary, it is an easier alternative to an advance directive. Nevertheless, it can serve to provide valuable information that may be crucial to doctors and family members in making decisions on behalf of patients.[76]

In addition to internet resources, visual media is also beginning to be used by individual physicians to facilitate advance care planning. Using video decision-making tools has helped patients discern minimally acceptable quality of life or function that can serve as an anchor point for decision-making around whether to accept treatment that may extend the patient's life without any improvement in the quality. Participants in a study who viewed a goals-of-care video, realistically depicting the burdens of various options in relation to the prospective benefits, were more likely to prefer comfort care to aggressive measures, avoid CPR, and be more certain of their decisions.[77]

A flurry of death-related parlor games is also appearing on the scene. For instance, the Conversation Game consists of thirty-six cards with short statements reflecting what people often consider important in their last days and a wild card that prompts more in-depth discussion about priorities and preferences at the end of life. Similarly, the Death Deck is a game that allows players to explore topics around death in a nonthreatening way, asking questions such as, "You get to relive one day in your life before you die, which one would it be?" Go Wish has players arrange cards with wishes listed on them, such as "to have my family with me," "not being short of breath," and "dying at home," according to what matters most. Heart2Hearts includes fifty-two conversation starters around decisions like whether the player would want a feeding tube if suffering from dementia. The board game Now and Then takes players on a journey through life, while having them confront decisions around the kind of death they are seeking. Some companies are expanding their products and addressing diversity needs by developing games in a variety of languages, including Chinese.[78]

These conversation starters build upon the idea of death cafés, introduced in England in 2011 by Jon Underwood, who was a follower of Swiss sociologist and anthropologist Bernard Crettaz. Crettaz called for "bringing death out of the silence" through conversations over food and drink. Taking place in coffee shops, church basements, and people's homes, nine years later, there are 11,500 death cafés in seventy-three countries. And while they, too, have had to move online due to COVID-19, their main website offers blogs, digital art galleries, quotes, support groups, and other resources related to death and bereavement.[79]

The appearance of death cafés coincided with Caitlin Doughty's founding of the Order of the Good Death and the YouTube channel "Ask a Mortician." Part of the "death positive movement," their site encompasses discussion prompts related to segregation and racism in cemeteries, home funerals, green death technology, conservation burials, and links to movies, podcasts, and books on death and dying.

The Order of Good Death maintains that the acceptance of death is natural, but the death anxiety in our modern culture is not. The tenets of the movement reflect the attitudes that hiding death and dying behind closed doors does more harm than good to society; the culture of silence should be broken through discussions, gatherings, art, innovation, and scholarship; talking about and engaging with the inevitability of death displays a natural curiosity about the human condition; and open, honest advocacy around death can make a difference and change the culture.[80]

Each of the efforts outlined at both the system-wide and individual patient-physician level can play a role in transforming cultural attitudes. In the process, they hold the potential to dramatically reduce patient suffering at the end of life.

CONCLUSION

When I taught at the Brown Medical School, I used my friend Al Killilea's book *The Politics of Being Mortal* in my courses on ethical issues in death and dying. Among the most important points he makes in his work is that it is not death we fear as much as it is "annihilation and the absurdity of a meaningless life."[81] For him, it is only through a recognition and acceptance of human interdependence that meaning can be given to both death and life. And it is only through greater candor about death that the anxieties and fears of citizens will be lessened, and meaningful dialogue will ensue.

In preparing my own pre-med and medical students at both Brown and the University of Rhode Island for grappling with these issues and for helping others confront the human condition, I would begin my section on death and the meaning of life by inviting them to give me the name, or any information really, about their maternal great-great-grandmothers. I taught four sections per semester—large classes of 120 students—and yet, not once, did anyone have the information. Perhaps this would be different today with the advent of ancestry.com and other genealogy databases. But, in every class I was able to say to them: "Here is a woman responsible for your very existence, and yet you can't even tell me her name. Is there any hope that 150 years from now anyone will know anything about you? And if not, does your life now really matter?"

It was a cruel thing to do, especially in the fall, as darkness descended early and students were preparing for the holiday break. When asked about my own view, I talked about meaning in my life coming from service to others and baseball, referring to an article by philosopher Morris Raphael Cohen, who recounted the Jewish American immigrant experience with the sport, suggesting it provided a mystic unity with something larger than themselves. My point with the exercise was to reinforce that the science they were studying would undoubtedly help us discover the causes and treatments of diseases such as cancer, Alzheimer's, and Parkinson's, but that it could not help us decide how to live our lives in the face of such diagnoses, determine whether there can ever be meaning in life given the inevitability of death, or speak to the experience of a mystic unity.

Indeed, until we are willing to have a national conversation about these issues and a more open treatment of death in relation to issues of racial and social justice, I suspect that many of my doctor's visits will continue to serve as ethics consults. For healthcare providers are likely to experience ever-increasing moral distress over how to abide by the Hippocratic Oath's enjoinder to first do no harm in a society in which death continues to be viewed as patently un-American.

2

ON SNOWFLAKES, CHILLY CLIMATES, AND SHOUTING TO BE HEARD

The Role of Liberal Education in Weathering Campus Storms

FREE SPEECH, EQUITY, AND INCLUSION

In 1998, when I was chair of the philosophy department at the University of Rhode Island (URI), there was a series of campus protests related to allegations of racism under the guise of free speech, ultimately leading to a takeover of the administration building, Taft Hall. The protests were sparked by an incident that occurred just before the December final exam period, when the student newspaper, the *Good Five Cent Cigar*, ran a nationally syndicated editorial cartoon as a filler. Appearing without commentary, the cartoon depicted a Black man carrying books attempting to enter a classroom. The White professor, standing behind a podium bearing the words "UT Law School," calls out, "If you're the janitor, please wait until after class to empty the trash. If you're one of our minority students, welcome!"

Two days after the appearance of the cartoon, student protestors from a Black activist group called the Brothers United for Action circulated a list of demands that included "a new campus newspaper that reflects a campus-wide commitment to ending racism, sexism, and homophobia, and promotes a vision of cultural empathy and understanding."[1] The managing editor of the paper responded by defending his selection and publication of the cartoon, maintaining that he "felt that the cartoon was clearly a worthwhile commentary in favor of affirmative action and minority rights."[2] He attributed anger over its content to confusion due to a lack of familiarity with the 1996 *Hopwood v. Texas* decision in which four White students who were rejected from the law school successfully challenged the institution's affirmative action policy in admissions on the grounds of equal protection. In the wake of that opinion, both UT president Robert Berdahl and system chancellor William Cunningham spoke out against the court's decision, with Berdahl predicting "the virtual resegregation of higher education."[3]

At the time, I happened to be teaching a mixed graduate/undergraduate-level course entitled "Race, Gender, and the Law," and my students were intimately acquainted with every aspect of the *Hopwood* case. Yet, many of them were either directly involved in the Brothers United protests or agreed with those who read the cartoon as conveying the message that students of color were neither welcome on campus nor deserving of a university education. They cited the lack of accompanying commentary and the timing of the cartoon's publication, a full year after the circuit court's decision, as evidence in support of their view.

The editor's rejoinder was: "This is always a timely issue. It is not like the Texas courts did something, made a decision, and it went away: the repercussions continue."[4] Reacting to the concerns, the *Cigar* ran the cartoon again, this time with an editorial response to the protests, explaining that the intention of the satirical cartoon was to show support for affirmative action. Protestors were not satisfied, pointing to the fact that only a month earlier, a racist message had been left on the answering machine in the Affirmative Action office. Even more egregious, at a Midnight Madness event during the previous basketball season—a season in which a group of students chanted racial epithets at some of the Black players—a White student urinated on an African American disc jockey. In the aftermath of these actions, the decision to run the cartoon took on a different meaning, and the Student Senate Executive Committee proposed a resolution calling for a formal apology by the editors. This coincided with a freeze by the Student Senate on funds allocated to the paper, pending an investigation into their finances.

While the Senate leaders disavowed any connection between the funding freeze and the protests, the newspaper staff regarded the actions as not only retributive but also as a violation of their First Amendment rights.[5] Their advisor, a journalism professor, joined faculty from philosophy, sociology, and politics in facilitating open forums centered on the questions of who gets to decide what constitutes racial offense and the circumstances, if any, whereby offense can serve as a legitimate liberty-limiting principle within the context of college campuses committed to the free exchange of ideas and to safeguarding the equality of educational opportunity.

More than two decades later, these same questions continue to be at the forefront of public discussion and private debate as pleas for the reform of institutional cultures through the elimination or racism, sexism, cis-sexism, homophobia, ableism, and other forms of hegemony persist and are played out on college and university campuses across the country. Nevertheless, there are stark differences in the nature and content of the discourse today. Issues of free speech at colleges and universities are no longer confined to what is said in classrooms and lecture halls, written in the student newspaper, or chalked on sidewalks—though as we have seen with the most recent presidential campaigns, such acts can create just as much campus strife, leading institutions to ban political chalk talk. Fueled by the advent of social media, roving strangers with targeted agendas troll websites and offer resources on how to construct sets of non-negotiable demands and solicit electronic votes of no confidence. Actions on one campus can instantaneously lead to a storm of protest activity in solidarity with those at colleges and universities across the nation, and commentary in online outlets frequently traverses boundaries, veering into genuine threats of harm.

Facebook, Instagram, YouTube, Reddit, and Twitter function as catalysts for the dissemination of political, social, and cultural ideologies, as well as for the rapid proliferation of both hateful rhetoric and massive disinformation campaigns. Yet, these tools for airing grievances and distributing propaganda have also shaped protest movements through ever-expanding modes of communication that document real and perceived injustices before they ever reach administrative offices. Three recent cases are emblematic of the power of social media in shaping the narrative, while showcasing the current complexities of balancing inclusion, equity, and freedom of expression.

The first case arose from outrage due to comments made on Twitter by University of Central Florida (UCF) psychology professor Charles Negy, author of *White Shaming: Bullying Based on Prejudice, Virtue Signaling, and Ignorance*. Negy tweeted: "Sincere question: If Afr. Americans as a group, had the same behavioral profile as Asian Americans (on average, performing the best academically, having the highest income, committing the lowest crime, etc.), would we still be proclaiming 'systemic racism' exists?" A year earlier, Negy had provoked similar fury in a tweet over the decision by another college to stop requiring standardized tests for admission. He wrote of the new policy: "It's the latest disingenuous ploy to admit more less-prepared African American and Hispanic students into a university for 'diversity.' Demanding less-prepared students improve their math and reading skills is too much to ask, apparently."[6]

Among the petitions that have appeared online calling for Negy's dismissal is one that has secured more than twenty-eight thousand signatures, asserting that his tweets go beyond viewpoint expression and translate into mistreatment in the classroom. While UCF posted on its official Twitter page that Negy's views are "completely counter to UCF's culture," the university's president, Alexander Cartwright, cited protections of tenure and the First Amendment in explaining to protestors the challenges of firing Negy for expressing his views—even racist ones. One student protestor responded to the administration by saying: "There needs to be a better system in place that would fire someone like this more immediately. As a Black woman, if it's not safe for me in a classroom, then where is it safe? . . . I'm paying a lot of money to come here. And I'm funding someone who makes other people, other students, feel small."[7] Another commented: "He is specifically targeting students of color. It's an issue of systemic racism. . . . You can speak your opinions, but not when it's hindering us in the classroom. I don't think our university should tolerate racism at the classroom level and making students feel uncomfortable."[8]

A second high-profile case involves marketing professor Joel Poor from the University of Missouri at Columbia, who was relieved of his teaching duties following comments he made in a virtual classroom setting. During introductions, the professor asked students where they were from. When one of the students reported being from Wuhan, China, Poor laughed and said, "Let me get my mask on." He then went on to welcome the student, offer any necessary assistance, including a bedroom in his home, and noted that while he had visited Shanghai and Chongqing, he had not had the pleasure of visiting Wuhan.[9] The exchange, which was captured in a one-minute video posted on social media, prompted demands for Poor's firing.

Just a few weeks earlier, a joint letter from the president and chancellors on each of the system's four campuses reaffirmed their shared commitment to racial justice, declaring: "Those who act with integrity have no patience for discrimination, no tolerance for hatred and do not condone an environment that is unsafe for those seeking or administering an education. . . . It is our responsibility . . . to steer our universities and our people through good and bad times with empathy, support and respect for all."[10] This was not new territory for the administrators, given that in 2015, the University of Missouri became a focus of racial-climate issues when protests and a hunger strike led to the resignation of the system president and the chancellor at the Columbia campus. Critics were now arguing that little had changed in the ensuing five years and that professed efforts to engage in antiracism had fallen short.

Though Poor publicly apologized for what he described as a joke taken out of context—one that was not intended to offend—a student group aimed at promoting racial justice, using the hashtag #Still Concerned, labeled Poor's comments "racist and xenophobic."[11] At the same time, defenders of Poor started an online petition, which quickly garnered more than five thousand signatures. The Young America's Foundation chimed in, calling the university's decision to remove Poor from the classroom "another example of the dangers of cancel culture" and warning that "this incident will have a chilling effect on free expression as professors intentionally restrict their own opinions and free speech in the wake of Mizzou's decision. Never bend a knee to the mob—it shows the tyrants-in-training who is truly running the school."[12]

The third case centers on University of Southern California's Greg Patton, a clinical business communication professor, who was removed from teaching his "Communication for Management" class for MBA students that was being taught via Zoom. Concerns were raised after a lecture was posted on Blackboard in which Patton uses a word taken from Mandarin, nèige (那个), in teaching a lesson on filler words, such as the use of "um" and "like" by English-language speakers. The word, which is pronounced "nay-ga," and often repeated in a sequence, means "that." Patton, who had been teaching in the Shanghai program for years without incident, was first alerted to perceived offense arising from his example when he was reading his midcourse evaluations. Three evaluations out of more than two hundred identified discomfort or hurt in response to hearing a word that sounded similar to an anti-Black racial slur in English.

Patton's case is reminiscent of the uproar created two decades ago at the University of Wisconsin when an English professor teaching Chaucer used "niggardly," a word whose meaning was unfamiliar to a Black student in the class.[13] Yet, unlike the Wisconsin case, in which the professor continued using the word even after he knew it was causing offense, Patton immediately decided to replace his example using the Mandarin word with one from Portuguese. Moreover, he issued both a written an apology to the class and a verbal one over Zoom the next morning. He followed up with an extensive written apology to the Graduate Association of the Marshall Business School, who represented the program in which the course was being taught.[14]

By then, a group of students identifying themselves as "Black MBA Candidates c/o 2022" had written a letter to the dean of the business school accusing Professor Patton of "negligence and disregard" and expressing dismay over what they considered a "grave and inappropriate" use of language. The students averred: "Our mental health has been affected. It is an uneasy feeling allowing him to have power over our grades. We would rather not take this course than to endure the emotional exhaustion of carrying on with an instructor that disregards cultural diversity and sensitivities and by extension creates an unwelcome environment for us Black students."[15] In response, the dean offered the aggrieved students the option of taking the rest of the three-week class as an independent study, having their work graded by a different professor, taking the course with another professor, or enrolling in another elective course. When some students rejected all of these options, the dean emailed the MBA class of 2022, notifying them that Professor Patton would no longer be teaching the class and that it was "simply unacceptable for faculty to use words in class that can marginalize, hurt and harm the psychological safety of our students." The dean added that he was "deeply saddened by this disturbing episode that has caused such anguish and trauma," but, unfortunately, "what happened cannot be undone."[16]

As this was unfolding, an online petition to reinstate Patton appeared, which collected more than nineteen thousand signatures. This coincided with a letter signed by nearly one hundred alumni of the business school, many of whom were from China, and who characterized the student complaint as a "spurious charge [that] has the additional feature of casting insult toward the Chinese language." Whereas Black students referenced the emotional impact of acts of anti-Black racism in America, the alumni invoked the devastating societal consequences of China's Cultural Revolution and the false accusations that were made against individuals in the name of the public good.[17]

In each of these cases, those asserting that the real harm is in deterring, suppressing, or punishing speech are pitted against those contending that the administration has violated the rights of students to a safe learning environment—one free from discrimination and intimidation. In addition to the First Amendment, the former often appeal to principles of academic freedom in condemning sanctions imposed on professors' speech both inside and outside of the classroom. A core principle of American higher education, academic freedom is grounded in the notion that the mission of colleges and universities, serving the public good through generating and conveying knowledge, depends upon the free exchange of ideas and the unfettered pursuit of the truth.

While statements regarding the concept of academic freedom vary from institution to institution, they are uniformly derived from a joint statement developed in 1940 by the American Association of Colleges and Universities and the American Association of University Professors. According to the "Statement of Principles on Academic Freedom and Tenure": "Teachers are entitled to full freedom in research and in the proliferation in the results, subject to the adequate performance of their other academic duties. . . . Teachers are entitled to freedom in the classroom in discussing their subject, but they should be careful not to introduce into their teaching controversial matter which has no relation to their subject."[18]

The protections of academic freedom in the classroom entail a wide range of activities, including testing, the distribution of reading lists, the development of coursework and syllabi, and the invitation of guest speakers. However, under this foundational statement, academic freedom extends to speech outside of the classroom, as well, reading: "College and University teachers are citizens, members of a learned profession, and officers of an educational institution. When they speak or write as citizens, they should be free from institutional censorship or discipline, but their special position in the community imposes special obligations. As scholars and educational officers, they should remember that the public may judge their profession and their institution by their utterances. Hence at all times, they should be accurate, should exercise appropriate restraint, should show respect for the opinions of others, and should make every effort to indicate that they are not speaking for the institution."[19] Protecting extramural speech is considered essential to the public purposes of the academy and to upholding the right of faculty members to remain faithful to their beliefs without fear of retaliation.

Nevertheless, academic freedom does not entitle professors to intimidate, threaten, harass, ridicule, or impose their views on students, leading to the debate over exactly which statements are protected under this principle. In the courts, the bar has been set high for those maintaining that speech in the classroom or on social media violates a duty of care for student well-being or infringes on the right to equal education. Under Title VI and Title IX of the Civil Rights Act, which charges colleges and universities with preventing a hostile learning environment, "harassing speech would need to be so severe, pervasive, and objectively offensive so as to jeopardize a student's equal access to the university before it could be actionable."[20]

The students in Professor Negy's case were making a further claim, however, that even if the speech he used failed to rise to the level of being severe, pervasive, or objectively offensive, the attitudes reflected by his words would make it impossible for him to discharge his duties as a professor. For, if brought into the classroom, these perceived racial biases would inevitably threaten equitable access to a safe learning environment, regardless of whether they actually influenced how he assessed students of color.

Similar concerns were raised in a more recent episode involving Jennifer Mosher, a biology professor at Marshall University. Mosher was placed on administrative leave following her comments around the refusal by some people at pro-Trump presidential campaign rallies to engage in social distancing or wear masks. Throughout the last stages of the 2020 campaign, the president was criticized for holding potential super-spreader events in which one person infects a disproportionately large number of individuals. By the time the campaign rallies took place, scientists had uncovered the increased risks for those attending functions where large crowds have congregated indoors and where people are shouting in close proximity to one another. Scientific models indicated that 10 to 20 percent of individuals have been responsible for 80 percent of the cases of COVID-19. Because the coronavirus differs from many other respiratory infections in that people infected may be asymptomatic for up to six days, scientists have warned against attending indoor gatherings of more than five individuals.[21]

Shortly after one of the first of these rallies, former presidential candidate Herman Cain, who was in attendance, contracted the coronavirus and died. Reports of several other attendees contracting the disease heightened concerns over the continuation of these types of political rallies. In discussing the continuous flouting of safety recommendations provided by doctors and the Centers for Disease Control based upon the latest research, Mosher admitted: "I've become the type of person where I hope they all get it and die. I'm sorry, but that's so frustrating—just—I don't know what else to do. You can't argue with them, you can't talk sense with them, um, I said to somebody yesterday I hope they all die before the election."[22] At the end of the forty-four-second clip, Mosher's acknowledges, "I really shouldn't be talking politics here."[23]

After a video of Mosher's comments went viral on social media, university officials responded with a statement that "The university does not support or condone the use of any of its educational platforms to belittle people or wish harm on those who hold differing political views."[24] Further, her suspension signals the administration's view that while Mosher's statements are protected in the public domain under the First Amendment as core political speech, they are not necessarily covered by the principles of academic freedom, especially if they are interpreted as failing to "exercise appropriate restraint" and "show respect for the opinions of others."

Thus, Pen America, a nonprofit organization that works to defend and celebrate free expression, makes clear in its latest campus free-speech guide that "Universities have an obligation to ensure that faculty can discharge their professional duties in a responsible, impartial way that gives students equal opportunities for success. If faculty speech impairs this sense of belonging or the equal treatment of particular segments of the campus population, it may be appropriate for leaders to distance themselves or condemn the speech and reassert the institution's values."[25]

Nonetheless, even while recognizing the potential negative effects for all students when a classroom dynamic devolves into one in which some students are left wondering whether a professor's views will influence the teaching and grading of the class, the organization asserts that "barring evidence that the speech in question has a clear and direct ramification on a professor's ability to fulfill their professional duties, the principle of academic freedom should be hewed to as a high standard."[26]

In the end, balancing appeals to freedom of expression in these cases with claims that allowing certain speech creates a hostile environment on campuses requires taking into account the broader cultural landscape—one in which there is a new permission structure for overt acts of racism and White supremacy and a growing societal response to acts of anti-Black racism.

A MOMENT OF RACIAL RECKONING

The public killing of an African American man, George Floyd, at the hands of Minneapolis police officers, broadcast for eight minutes and forty-six seconds in a continuous loop over television and social media, was a turning point in what has become a cultural spectacle of Black death. Floyd's murder took place amid the backdrop of a nation reeling from the worst global pandemic in over a century—disparately impacting Black, Latinx, and American Indian communities—and from an economic recession leading to the highest unemployment rate since the Great Depression. As people took to the streets in Black Lives Matter protests across the country, it became clear that Mr. Floyd's death had sparked a moment of racial reckoning in America.

The toppling of Confederate monuments and the removal of the Confederate battle emblem from the Mississippi state flag coincided with NASCAR banning Confederate symbols from appearing at their races and events.[27] NFL commissioner Roger Goodell apologized for the policy he enacted two years earlier that barred kneeling during the national anthem, encouraging all to speak out and peacefully protest, and saying he should have listened to players earlier. At the time, however, there was no explicit mention of former San Francisco 49ers' quarterback Colin Kaepernick, who was blacklisted for spearheading a movement by taking a knee during the national anthem to protest police brutality against Black Americans. Instead, Goodell announced that "Lift Every Voice," known as the Black national anthem, would be played before every football game.[28]

Nike, which was widely boycotted for making Colin Kaepernick the face of their thirtieth-anniversary "Just Do It!" campaign, imposing the slogan "Believe in something. Even if it means sacrificing everything" over his image, released a new advertisement five days after a White police officer kneeled on Floyd's neck until he died. White text flashed across a black screen, encouraging viewers to break their silence, stop making excuses, and be the change, with the words: "For once, don't do it. Don't pretend there's not a problem in America. Don't turn your back on racism. Don't accept innocent lives being taken from us."[29]

ViacomCBS networks MTV, Comedy Central, and VH1 aired the words "I can't breathe," with an audio clip of the sounds of breathing in the background that spanned the amount of time George Floyd was pleading for his life. The spot enjoined viewers to text "Color of Change" in support of the fight against racial injustice. Ben & Jerry's, which had already taken a public stance in support of Black Lives Matter four years earlier, posted a message on its website calling for the dismantling of White supremacy and detailed four specific action steps to address racism.[30]

Companies, including PayPal, Disney, Warner Bros., Sony, Comcast, Verizon, Pokémon, Lego, Riot Games, DoorDash, TikTok, Facebook, Amazon, YouTube, Microsoft, Target, Google, Coca-Cola, and Bank of America, pledged millions of dollars in support of organizations working to stem racial inequities. Some of these companies examined the ways in which their own practices and policies were complicit in the perpetuation of structural racism and subsequently announced changes. Walmart, Walgreens, and CVS ended the practice of displaying beauty products for Blacks and other people of color in locked cases and committed to increasing the product selection aimed at serving diverse patrons. Beauty-products giant Sephora went further by being the first retailer to sign the 15 percent pledge, in which 15 percent of the shelf space, representing the percentage of Black people in the

United States, is designated for selling products from Black-owned businesses.[31]

Quaker Oats, owner of the 131-year-old Aunt Jemima brand, made headlines with reports that the company would be changing its packaging, which was steeped in the nineteenth-century Mammy stereotype. Surrounded by criticism that their imagery similarly relied on racist tropes of minstrelsy, Cream of Wheat, Uncle Ben's, and Mrs. Butterworth's all announced that they would be undergoing a review of their packaging and marketing. By then, Land O' Lakes had begun a quiet phaseout of Mia, the Indian maiden who has appeared kneeling by a blue lake on the side of their boxes of butter since 1921.[32]

Adobe, All State, Altria, Best Buy, JC Penny, Lyft, Postmates, RX Bar, Spotify, Twitter, and Square were among the companies designating Juneteenth as a paid holiday for their employees. Prior to the national attention brought to what is also known as Freedom Day, many Americans had never heard about the celebration commemorating June 19, 1865, when Union soldiers, led by General Gordon Granger, arrived in Galveston, Texas, and delivered the news that President Lincoln had signed the Emancipation Proclamation two and a half years earlier on January 1, 1863, the war had ended, and the enslaved were now free.

Within six weeks of Mr. Floyd's death, multinational delivery service company FedEx notified the Washington football team that unless the name "Redskins" was dropped, they would remove their signage from the stadium and end the $205 million naming-rights deal six years before it was due to expire. Within a day, team owner Dan Snyder announced that they were undergoing "a thorough review of the name," and ten days later Washington reported that they would be retiring their eighty-seven-year-old name and logo. Just seven years earlier, when asked about the use of Native American mascots and charges that the team's name was a racial slur, Snyder asserted definitively, "We'll never change the name. It's that simple. NEVER," adding "you can use caps."[33]

While Snyder's change of heart was stunning for many, it was nothing compared to the unprecedented moment in U.S. professional sports when players in the NBA, WNBA, Major League Baseball, and Major League Soccer, recognizing the power of the bottom line, took a collective stand against police brutality and racial injustice by boycotting playoff and regular-season games in response to the shooting of Jacob Blake, a Black man shot in the back seven times by police in Kenosha, Wisconsin.[34] Two days later, thousands gathered at the base of the Lincoln Memorial in renewed calls for racial justice in the place where Dr. Martin Luther King Jr. delivered his iconic "I Have a Dream Speech." The "Get Your Knee Off Our Necks" Commitment March, named in honor of George Floyd, took place on the fifty-seventh anniversary of the March on Washington for Jobs and Justice and on the sixty-fifth anniversary of the lynching of fourteen-year-old Emmett Till—an event that catalyzed the civil rights movement.[35]

CAMPUS RESPONSES

During this same time period, colleges and universities across the nation started opening for the fall semester, and presidents and chancellors took pains to assure students, faculty, and staff of their commitment to diversity and inclusion and to the safety and well-being of all members of their communities. Many had already joined business leaders, politicians, and celebrities over the summer in issuing statements condemning racism and police brutality. Yet, as fast as these letters to the community appeared in press releases and on college and university websites, critiques surfaced by those who perceived the missives as mere performative acts, amounting to nothing more than platitudes. For Carnegie Mellon professors Jason England and Richard Purcell, "statements in response to the killing of George Floyd reflect[ed] an unholy alchemy of risk management, legal liability, and trustee anxiety"[36] as opposed to strategies and tactics for institutional transformation grounded in an acknowledgment of anti-Black racism and White supremacy.

The hashtag #BlackintheIvory, shining a spotlight on racism in academia, exploded, and college and university administrators were called upon with increasing frequency to recognize and redress the ways in which higher education reinforces structural racism, as reflected by the lack of diversity among faculty and administrators, insufficient funding for Black and other ethnic studies programs, the absence of student input on campus police budgets, the omission of databases chronicling racial bias incidents by officers, and the continued presence of racist iconography on campuses—from Confederate statues to the names of buildings, centers, and the institutions themselves.[37]

As campus leaders were coming under heightened scrutiny, the American Association of Colleges and Universities collaborated with ABC Insights to conduct a survey of college and university presidents to explore how they were responding to these calls for racial justice and the mandate to address anti-Black racism within their institutions and on their campuses. Administered between June 25 and July 12, 2020, to members of AAC&U's Presidents' Trust, a diverse network of college and university leaders who are committed to advancing the vision, values, and practices that connect liberal education with the needs of an increasingly diverse student body, a global workforce, and thriving communities, the survey elicited a 44.7 percent response rate. A majority of the 119 respondents (55 percent) were presidents of four-year private colleges or universities with fewer than five thousand students. Presidents of medium-to-large public universities were the next-largest group of respondents (38 percent). Community college presidents of medium-to-large institutions were the smallest group of respondents, comprising 19 percent of the total sample.[38]

Eighty percent of presidents believed it was either "likely" or "very likely" that student activism related to issues of racial justice would occur on their campuses in the fall and reported being engaged in both short-term and long-term planning to address issues of systemic racism. Whereas short-term planning was focused on initiating dialogue and communication across stakeholders, long-term tactics included strategic hiring and curriculum reform, as well as the broad interrogation of institutional practices and policies to identify and counter inequities. The actions undertaken indicated an understanding that campuses must be willing to engage in truth-telling conversations about the existence and persistence of inequities, that equity goals need to be embedded within the strategic priorities of all institutions, that racialized practices marginalizing students of color must be confronted directly, and that preparation to address structural and systemic racism must be a core component of a liberal education.[39]

Indeed, taking direct aim at educational disparities and patterns of systemic disadvantage—especially those resulting from historical and contemporary effects of racism—and making equity a pervading focus of educational reform and innovation requires moving beyond the goals of access and compositional diversity to design and deliver experiences that support the success of all students.[40] This, in turn, requires making colleges and universities places of welcome and belonging.

SNOWFLAKES, TRIGGER WARNINGS, AND SAFE SPACES

Steeped in debates over trigger warnings, safe spaces, and free-speech zones, the subsequent discourse about what exactly such a learning environment should look like has been dominated by accusations of rampant political correctness and groupthink in service to a progressive, liberal agenda, countered by protestors demanding that college and university officials be held accountable for the participation in, and perpetuation of, structures of oppression.[41] Four years ago, John Ellison, the dean of students at the University of Chicago, created a firestorm with his welcome letter to the class of 2020, which stated: "Our commitment to academic freedom means that we do not support so-called trigger warnings, we do not cancel invited speakers because their topics might prove controversial and we do not condone the creation of intellectual safe spaces where individuals can retreat from ideas and perspectives at odds with their own."[42]

While many, including conservative columnist George Will, who has described this generation of college students as "such delicate snowflakes that they melt at the mere mention of even a potential abrasion of their sensibilities,"[43] found the message heartening, others decried it as undermining inclusion and limiting academic freedom by discouraging specific educational practices aimed at fostering diversity and student success. For instance, one contributor to the blog *The Good Enough Professor* characterized Dean Ellison's statement as a solution in search of a problem, positioning the challenges to free speech as "mythical." The blogger suggested instead that political leaders and influencers begin attending to the genuine threats to higher education and posted a list that included declining state support, the reduction of higher education to job training, student debt, and the overreliance on adjunct professors.

Countering the rhetoric deriding faculty and administrators for coddling students, the post delineates what should not be considered a threat to freedom of inquiry, such as "professors' efforts to prevent bigoted students from derailing discussion; the acknowledgment that traumatized students may find some material difficult"; and "events, spaces, organizations that give students who have, as a group, been historically excluded from certain institutions the opportunity—if they wanted to have community and a sense of belonging at those institutions."[44] It concludes with a list of phenomena that, in the experience of this professor of twelve years, do not actually exist in the academy, such as "institutionally enforced expectations that faculty not talk about certain things; institutionally enforced expectations that students be allowed to opt out of anything that makes them uncomfortable;

institutionally enforced expectations that students be protected from disturbing ideas; and the large-scale excision of intellectually viable yet controversial subject matter from college curricula."[45]

Unfortunately, the framing of debates over freedom of expression on campuses has frequently fallen prey to those with a partisan agenda, leading to the perpetuation of stereotypes and the proliferation of rhetoric often disconnected from reality. Echoing George Will's sentiments at a forum sponsored by the conservative group Turning Point USA, President Trump's former attorney general Jeffery Sessions warned: "Through 'trigger warnings' about 'microaggressions,' cry closets, 'safe spaces,' optional exams, therapy goats, and grade inflation, too many schools are coddling our young people and actively preventing them from scrutinizing the validity of their beliefs. That is the exact opposite of what they are supposed to do." He went on to say: "After the 2016 election, for example, they held a 'cry-in' at Cornell, they had therapy dogs on campus at the University of Kansas, and Play-Doh and coloring books at the University of Michigan. Students at Tufts were encouraged to 'draw about their feelings.' Rather than molding a generation of mature and well-informed adults, some schools are doing everything they can to create a generation of sanctimonious, sensitive, supercilious snowflakes. That is a disservice to their students and a disservice to this nation."[46]

Along the same lines, President Trump's secretary of education, Betsy DeVos, speaking to students in attendance at the Conservative Political Action Conference, exhorted: "The fight against the education establishment extends to you too. The faculty, from adjunct professors to deans, tell you what to do, what to say, and more ominously, what to think. They say that if you voted for Donald Trump, you're a threat to the university community. But the real threat is silencing the First Amendment rights of people with whom you disagree."[47]

Based in part on these characterizations, since 2017 more than thirty states have introduced legislation related to campus free speech, and as Pen America observes, "The intrusion of lawmakers into college and university governance risks further politicizing an already polarized campus atmosphere."[48] These bills range from a proposal in Arizona that would prohibit offering any class or activity that promotes "division, resentment, or social justice toward a race, gender, religion, political affiliation, social class or other class of people" to an Arkansas measure seeking to prohibit any curricula that contain writings by or about historian Howard Zinn. Many of these legislative proposals were influenced by model legislation, introduced in the same year by the Goldwater Institute with the intent of preventing liberal bias within America's public university systems.[49]

The proposed legislation proscribes disinviting speakers, no matter how controversial; establishes a system of disciplinary sanctions for anyone who interferes with the free-speech rights of others; allows the recovery of court costs and attorney's fees by anyone whose rights have been improperly infringed upon; authorizes a special subcommittee of the university board of trustees to issue a report to the public, the trustees, the governor, and the legislature on the administrative handling of free-speech issues; reaffirms the principle that universities ought to remain neutral at the institutional level on issues of public controversy to encourage the broadest range of opinion and dialogue; and calls for creating and informing all students of an official university policy that affirms the importance of free expression while nullifying existing restrictive speech codes.[50]

In addition to the proliferation of state legislation that emerged from the Goldwater Institute proposal, the principles underlying the plan have been employed at the federal level to justify a variety of measures, including threats by the Department of Education under the Trump administration to withhold federal grant money from Middle East studies programs that are perceived by the department as advancing an ideological agenda by promoting "a positive view of Islam while virtually ignoring Judaism, Christianity and other religions." Hence, the Duke-UNC Consortium for Middle East Studies was ordered to revise its offerings or risk losing a $235,000 federal grant. Critics have argued that this move by the administration not only violates academic freedom but takes the politicization of college and university campuses to a new and disturbing level.[51]

Besides concerns over the level of government intrusion into curricula at colleges and universities, detractors of any proposal that mandates neutrality on the part of institutions of higher education related to issues of public concern wonder what applying these principles would mean when to comes to teaching topics such as climate change, evolution, the efficacy of vaccines, or the evils of slavery. Requiring neutrality in these instances would undermine the mission and purposes of higher education. In teaching and research, and when students are engaged in classroom discussions, taking exams, and writing essays, not all perspectives are considered uniformly valid. Content and viewpoint are dictated to the extent that one's contributions must not only be relevant, but they must also demonstrate knowledge, skills, and competencies agreed upon by experts in the field.

Notwithstanding these challenges, President Trump issued an executive order in 2019 entitled "Improving Free Inquiry, Transparency, and Accountability at Colleges and Universities." The order mandated that colleges and universities enforce free inquiry or run the risk of losing public funds. In a speech from the White House, surrounded by more than one hundred student activists who claimed that their conservative viewpoints were being suppressed on their college campuses, the president pronounced: "Under the guise of 'speech codes' and 'safe spaces' and 'trigger warnings,' these universities have tried to restrict free thought, impose total conformity, and shut down the voices of great young Americans like those here today. These are great people."[52]

The presidential order directed federal agencies to "take appropriate steps" to ensure that colleges receiving federal research funds "promote free inquiry." However, because public colleges are already legally bound to meet these dictates under the First Amendment, and private colleges will only be required to "comply with their stated institutional policies regarding free inquiry," the order has functioned more as a political statement than substantive legislation. This does not mean that the executive order has been dismissed as inconsequential by college and university leaders. In particular, the broadness and vagueness of the legislation raised concerns around the insufficient guidance provided to administrators in the face of colleges and universities being threatened with the loss of federal funds.

Consider, for instance, the following dilemmas. Amid rising tensions on American college campuses following student protests in Hong Kong, an op-ed entitled "I Am from Hong Kong, Not China," written by a student at Emerson College in Boston, was posted on Facebook by one of her classmates. Alongside the post was the response: "Whomever opposes my greatest China, no matter how far they are, must be executed." In the days that followed, the author of the op-ed was subjected to expletives and lewd gestures by Chinese students on campus.[53] These incidents, and similar ones taking place on college and university campuses across the country, prompt a consideration of the point at which the exercise of speech becomes a genuine threat and how college officials should respond to this type of post.

And, what are we to say about the free-expression rights of students like those at Wesleyan University who distributed fliers portraying a professor as a sex offender, sexual predator, and promoter of sexual violence, after he accused them of crossing the line by applying these labels to the president and provost for their perceived mishandling of sexual harassment cases at the inception of the #MeToo movement?[54] College officials have been forced to rethink issues of liability as they pertain to students' free expression following the decision by an Ohio jury to order Oberlin College to pay more than $11 million in damages to owners of a local bakery who charged that college students interfered with their business, engaged in libel, and inflicted emotional distress on them. Oberlin students began protesting the bakery following the arrest of three Black students accused of shoplifting. Though the students confessed and signed a statement denying that the incident was race-based, protests persisted, accusing the owners of White supremacy and handing out pamphlets entreating prospective customers not to buy from them. A dean, who informed law enforcement officers in advance of the protest and who approved the use of university funds to buy gloves for those participating, was accused of encouraging the demonstrations. From the university's perspective, she was simply ensuring the safety of students during the exercising of their legal rights—the very rights at the basis of the president's executive order.[55]

In addition, while the executive order sought "to promote free and open debate on college and university campuses" and "to avoid creating environments that stifle competing perspectives, thereby potentially impeding beneficial research and undermining learning," it remained silent on the impact of state campus carry laws that allow concealed weapons in classrooms and residence halls. Research presented at the American Educational Research Association, following a surge in campus carry legislation, indicated that 50 percent of the faculty surveyed reported that their "ability to teach controversial or emotionally charged topics will be negatively impacted." The greatest impact was reportedly on faculty who identified as Asian. The fears of many of these faculty members were captured in a PowerPoint presentation given on the floor of the Faculty Senate at the University of Houston by professor and Senate chair Jonathan Snow. Snow made national headlines when he advised his colleagues to "Be careful in discussing sensitive topics; drop sensitive topics from your curriculum; not 'go there' if you sense anger; limit student access off hours; go to appointment-only office hours; only meet 'that student' in controlled circumstances."[56] Given their chilling effect, should campus carry laws be viewed as having violated the federal mandate issued by President Trump?

Adding to the confusion, the former president's free-speech mandate seems straightforwardly inconsistent with a more recent executive order circumscribing any claims that "the existence of a State of Israel is a racist endeavor." By labeling such speech a violation of Title VI of the Civil Rights Act of 1964, which prohibits discrimination on the basis of race, color, or national origin by any program or activity receiving federal financial assistance, President Trump drew criticism for conflating anti-Semitism with anti-Zionism, while posing new challenges for college leaders who must safeguard freedom of expression and concomitantly prohibit anti-Israeli boycotts and pro-Palestinian sentiments as anti-Semitic.

This was the challenge in 2015 when a group of pro-Palestinian students at CUNY's Hunter College, who were part of a protest against rising tuition, began shouting, "Long live the intifada" and intoning that the Zionist administration was to blame for a recent spike in costs.[57] More recently, two Brooklyn College volleyball athletes took a knee rather than stand during the playing of the Israeli national anthem, broadcast at a game against Yeshiva University. Would curtailing the speech of the Hunter students or the actions of the Brooklyn players under this regulation comport with the law, or would it risk the loss of federal funds? The juxtaposition of these two orders invites differing interpretations as to how college leaders should proceed.

Furthermore, opponents of President Trump's executive order argue that more egregious than its failure to provide direction is the apparent design to protect only certain speech—namely speech representing views that are ideologically aligned with those of the administration. When the rollout of the executive order took place, Trinity University president Patricia McGuire immediately pointed to disparities in whose rights were protected under the legislation, asking:

> Where were all of the African American students who suffer racial slurs and horrific threats on campuses every day? Where were the Latinos, the Dreamers, the LGBTQ students who often endure egregious hostility and intimidation during their college years?
>
> ... He said at the ceremony that this order is the beginning of a more aggressive stance to protect student rights. Has the president spoken as boldly about protecting the rights of students of color on campus? Does his freedom of speech order cover the myriad displays

of nooses, bananas, swastikas, blackfaces, N-word scrawls and other racially offensive expressions that some students suffer regularly?

... Trump lifts up the "brave" anti-abortion cross planter who was simply told to include an explanatory sign on her display, but he never extolled Heather Heyer's bravery for giving her life as part of her exercise of freedom of speech. Trump mocks "trigger warnings" while soothing the valentine maker who was only allowed to distribute her "Jesus Loves You" cards in a specific place on campus, even as he says not a word of care or concern for those who suffer not only taunts but also real assaults at the hands of white supremacists, neo-Nazis and the assorted other contemptible hate groups that operate with gleeful insouciance in the Trump era.[58]

As early as 2017, red flags were raised regarding alleged attempts by President Trump to restrict speech on partisan grounds. Reminiscent of comedian George Carlin's infamous skit "Seven Words You Can Never Say on Television," anonymous sources within the Centers for Disease Control reported that they were instructed by the Trump administration to avoid using a list of seven words and phrases in Health and Human Services agencies' budget-planning documents. The identified words were "vulnerable," "entitlement," "diversity," "transgender," "fetus," "evidence-based," and "science-based," and while the leakers of the directive said no guidance was offered regarding the other words, they suggested that "evidence-based" and "research-based" should be replaced with, "the CDC bases its recommendations on science in consideration with community standards and wishes."[59]

Three years later there continued to be consternation with respect to whose speech was protected and whether the protection offered met the demands of a more just and equitable society. Two months after a July 2020 tweet in which the president reaffirmed his distress over what he termed "radical left indoctrination" on campuses and threatened to remove nonprofit colleges and universities from tax-exempt status, he issued another executive order with potential widespread implications for the higher education community.[60] This executive order prohibited federal contractors and institutions receiving federal grants from engaging in forms of diversity, inclusion, and bias training that are not approved by the government. The federal policy adjured grantees and contractors "not to promote race or sex stereotyping or scapegoating," and in the case of contractors, forbid them from trying to "inculcate such views in their employees."[61]

These prohibitions followed a previous executive order disallowing the same type of training, which the administration accused of pushing a liberal, progressive agenda, at federal agencies. In both instances, agencies may not implement workplace training programs that include the concepts that (1) one race is inherently superior to another race; (2) an individual, by virtue of his or her race or sex, is inherently racist, sexist, or oppressive, whether consciously or unconsciously; (3) an individual should be discriminated against or receive adverse treatment solely or partly because of his or her race or sex; (4) members of one race cannot or should not attempt to treat others without respect to race or sex; (5) an individual's moral character is necessarily determined by his or her race or sex; (6) an individual should feel discomfort, guilt, anguish, or any form of psychological distress on account of his or her race or sex; (7) meritocracy, or traits such as hard work ethic, are racist or sexist, or were created by a particular race to oppress another race; or that (8) it is appropriate to assign fault, blame, or bias to a race or sex, or to members of a race or sex because of their race or sex.[62]

The order required contractors to post these guidelines in a prominent location in the office building and online and to include them in all subcontract awards. It also directed the Office of Federal Contract Compliance Programs to establish a hotline and investigate programs that have been reported as noncompliant, which can result in the termination, cancellation, and debarring of contracts. While the executive order did not prevent contractors from engaging in training and other activities that promote racial, cultural, and ethnic diversity in a manner consistent with the guidelines, it was designed to ban antibias training such as Robin DiAngelo's White Fragility workshops that focus on implicit bias. DiAngelo's brand of antibias training is wildly popular at colleges and universities and now permeates institutions of every type across the country.

In fact, ten days after the killing of George Floyd, Speaker of the House Nancy Pelosi held a Democratic Caucus discussion on race, facilitated by DiAngelo, via conference call. DiAngelo's trenchant message—"For all the white people listening right now, thinking I am not talking to you. I am looking directly in your eyes and saying, 'It *is* you'"—makes clear that anti-Black bias in America cannot be addressed until every White person engages in self-examination around the question of what it means to be White.[63]

President Trump's attack on this type of bias training occurred at the same time the Department of Education launched an investigation into Princeton University, following a statement by the university's president, Christopher Eisgruber, in which he acknowledged the unremitting damage of structural racism and the ways in which racist assumptions remain embedded within his institution. As a result of the investigation, Princeton was required to demonstrate its compliance with federal antidiscrimination law, or risk penalties and the removal of federal funds.

Cries of concern over the move by the Department of Education arose immediately, contending that the probe constituted an "unwarranted, unprecedented and politically motivated intrusion into the private university." More than eighty leaders of colleges, universities, and higher education associations were signatories to a letter calling for a halt to the investigation, applauding Princeton's courage in grappling honestly with our nation's history of racism. Such exercises, they insist, should not be regarded as inconsistent with protecting individuals from discrimination under the Civil Rights Act.[64]

In addition, some wonder what happened to President Trump's espoused commitment to safeguarding a diversity of perspectives when he threatened to remove funding from public schools that teach the 1619 Project—a Pulitzer Prize–winning series of articles by the *New York Times* arguing that the year 1619, when slave ships first arrived in the American colonies, should mark the beginning of a nation built around the ideal of slavery rather than liberty.[65] After all, if the proclaimed intent of the executive order was to avoid stifling competing perspectives, even liberal perspectives deserve a full hearing. Yet, the administration called for a "pro-American curriculum" that "celebrates the truth about our nation's great history" to be taught in schools, replacing one that the former president characterized as promoting "left-wing rioting and mayhem."[66] Citing the White House directive for federal agencies to cancel race-related training sessions it calls "un-American propaganda," the Princeton inquiry, and threats to the 1619 Project, the American Educational Research Association and the National Academy of Education wrote in a joint statement, "We need educational systems that are not politicized and censored, but rather seek the truth by exploring even the most difficult truths."[67]

The contradictions inherent in these conflicting executive orders and their implementation have led to charges that previous federal legislation and much pending state legislation to safeguard speech on college campuses is not aimed at protecting speech across the political spectrum but rather illustrates the extent to which free speech has become increasingly weaponized in service to a partisan agenda. The examples raised are also emblematic of a distinctive shift regarding appeals to the First Amendment.

As Michigan law professor Catharine MacKinnon observes in her collection of essays *The Free Speech Century*: "Once a defense of the powerless, the First Amendment over the last hundred years has mainly become a weapon of the powerful. Legally, what was, toward the beginning of the 20th century, a shield for radicals, artists and activists, socialists and pacifists, the excluded and the dispossessed, has become a sword for authoritarians, racists and misogynists, Nazis and Klansmen, pornographers and corporations buying elections."[68]

Nonetheless, this transition in the way that the First Amendment has been used should not obscure the fact that there is a political agenda at play on both sides of the debate over the scope of free speech on college campuses. In his book *What Snowflakes Get Right*, Ulrich Baer tackles the issue of weaponized speech, asserting: "Let's be clear here: trigger warnings, speech codes and safe spaces are intended to afford all students, and especially minorities, equal learning opportunities. Their intent is not censorship, as is often asserted in the hunt for motives. But their motive is indeed political, as many critics of such rules insist. Equality concerns are always political. The debate is whether the new rules improve or worsen the status quo."[69]

For Baer, what has changed over time is not just the nature of the appeals to free speech but also how students respond and why. He contends:

> The students take seriously the self-evident truth that once
> admitted to the university, as far as group belonging, they have
> a right to equal participation. They do not accept that they must
> defend a neo-Nazi's right to speak who disputes Jewish, Black, and
> other minority students' right to exist. They also do not accept at face
> value the hypocrisy of organizations who defend a neo-Nazi's right
> to speech, ostensibly to uphold his constitutional rights against state
> suppression, and at the same time submit legislative bills mandating
> penalties for those who exercise their right to political protest. Such
> selective and dishonest application of constitutionally guaranteed
> rights reveals the intent of subjugating others, most often racial
> minorities and women, under the weaponized idea of free speech.[70]

These attitudes are captured in findings from a variety of studies that ask students about the degree to which they believe free speech, diversity, and inclusion should be protected and how they would weigh these values in cases of conflict.

A 2017 Knight Foundation study of U.S. college students showed that of the 3,014 students surveyed, 89 percent valued free-speech rights, with more than one-half identifying free speech as "extremely important" to democracy and approximately one-third citing these rights as "very important." Even so, the students were in favor of restrictions on free speech when exercising their rights involved hate speech or the wearing of stereotypical costumes that could cause offense.[71] In fact, 48 percent were supportive of "instituting speech codes of conduct that restrict offensive or biased speech on campus that would be permitted in society more generally."[72]

In the same study, 56 percent of the respondents believed that protecting free-speech rights is extremely important to democracy, and 52 percent held the belief that promoting a diverse and inclusive society is extremely important to democracy. Yet, when asked to prioritize, students gave preference to diversity and inclusion over free speech by a margin of 53 percent to 46 percent. A 2018 survey conducted by the Foundation for Individual Rights in Education (FIRE) revealed similar results. Seventy-five percent of those surveyed were convinced that students should have the right to free speech on campuses, even when what was being said is offensive to others. At the same time, they prioritized "promoting an inclusive environment" over protecting the free-speech rights of students.[73]

Findings from a further study undertaken in 2017 by the Buckley Center offer a possible explanation. Of the eight hundred student respondents, 81 percent agreed with the statement that "words can be a form of violence."[74] If students are convinced that beyond inciting violence, speech can cause actual harm, and not just discomfort or offense, it is understandable why they may seek to restrict certain expressions to protect others.[75] Though the issue of whether speech can ever constitute violence, beyond stress that leads to illness, remains widely contested, there is support for the students' viewpoint coming from a statement by Sandra Shullman, president of the American

Psychological Association. Shullman draws attention to the growing research around the ways in which racism, including racist speech, can contribute to psychological and physical harm, stating: "We are living in a racism pandemic, which is taking a heavy psychological toll on our African American citizens. The health consequences are dire. Racism is associated with a host of psychological consequences, including depression, anxiety and other serious, sometimes debilitating conditions, including post-traumatic stress disorder and substance use disorders. Moreover, the stress caused by racism can contribute to the development of cardiovascular and other physical diseases."[76]

If this is the case, even those who adhere to John Stuart Mill's philosophy of extreme liberalism, in which the harm principle is the only legitimate liberty-limiting principle, should countenance possible restrictions on speech. In fact, campus leaders need to resolve disputes over hateful speech within the context of emerging scientific evidence on the physical damage exposure to racism inflicts on brains and bodies. This must also be done with the knowledge that there has been "a marked rise in reports of hateful expression since 2016, including racist screeds, hate motivated violence, anti-Semitic symbols, and white supremacist propaganda," on campuses, fueling greater anxiety around issues of race.[77]

Increasingly, there is a blurring of protected speech and intimidation, especially when communicated over social media. When I was a college president, I routinely received demands from individuals in the extramural community to sanction faculty members who had taken political stances at odds with the views of those writing to me. These ultimatums were often accompanied by the addresses of the faculty members and the names of the schools their children attended. The lists were also made public by groups such as Turning Point USA, which established a Professor Watchlist in a campaign that has encouraged Internet trolls to engage in acts of harassment in an all-out culture war against "the liberal professoriate."

TRANSCENDING IDENTITY POLITICS

Tensions between those who claim that the right to free expression on campuses should not be at the expense of equality or human dignity and those who maintain that liberalism is both killing liberal education and threatening our democracy ultimately hinge on identity politics. Student protests around a wide range of diversity and inclusion issues offer a counternarrative to the dominant discourse that has traditionally marginalized the voices of women, students and faculty of color, religious and ethnic minorities, and members of the LGBTQ community. Like those who blocked recruiters from campuses during the Vietnam War, or engaged in sit-ins and freedom rides during the civil rights movement, these protestors regard their actions as justified on the grounds of necessity and attempts to stop them as further silencing the most vulnerable members of society and their allies.[78]

These protests also highlight the fact that the conclusions we draw regarding whether arguments and assertions in support of limiting speech are rational and warranted depend, in part, on whose stories are being told and who is doing the speaking. I was reminded that the burdens of free expression are not borne equally by all members of the community on a personal level after a controversial decision was made by the school board of the high school from which I graduated. Killingly High, located in a small town in northeastern Connecticut, is built on land once inhabited by the Nipmuc, Mohegan, and Mashantucket Pequot tribes. The athletic teams are known as the Killingly "Redmen," or alternatively the "Redgals." My alma mater received a raft of national attention when it became the first institution in the country to relinquish and then reappropriate what many consider to be a racist mascot.

In July 2019, the Democratic-controlled school board voted to replace the name "Redmen," adopted in 1939, with the "Red Hawks," deeming the former racially offensive. In November, a newly elected Republican-controlled board that had campaigned on the promise of reversing the mascot decision kept their word. During a five-hour open meeting of the board, not one person spoke in favor of returning to the name "Redmen," whereas a long line of students, administrators, coaches, and Native American community members raised their voices in opposition.[79] One of the board members, who had previously served as the vice president for the American Guard in Connecticut, cited as a hate group by the Southern Poverty Law Center, argued that "the renaming of the Redmen was the result of the 'radical left agenda of the town Democrats.'"[80] He insisted that voters should have the right to decide whether the mascot is racist, though his Democratic counterpart argued that a majority-White town should not have a referendum on what's racist and what's not.

Before making the decision to change their name to the Red Hawks, the previous board consulted with local Native American councils. Apart from the problem inherent in having any American Indian person as a mascot, something the American Psychological Association called for an end to in 2005, based on an extensive body of research indicating that racial stereotypes and inaccurate representations harm Native young people's self-esteem and social identity, a member of the Nipmuc Nation Tribal Council claimed that the image used by the town of Killingly was cartoonish and sacrilegious, stating: "That is regalia worn in prayer, in ceremonies. It doesn't belong on a football helmet."[81]

After the vote to reclaim the image, the board sought to appease angry citizens by forming two subcommittees—one to add a Native American component to the curriculum with lessons on why racist speech and actions are unacceptable and a second charged with redesigning the mascot image to avoid insensitive caricatures. A current board member, himself Native American, maintained: "It's never been racist or derogatory against Native Americans. . . . This is a melting pot. We take what's best and incorporate it into our culture. That's what Killingly did. They took something that is honorable and respectful and celebrated that."[82] By contrast, in response to the contention that the mascot is an attempt to honor Native Americans, the Tribal Council representative asserted: "It is a matter of perception that it honors us. And you can't honor someone if they don't want it. On behalf of the Nipmuc Nation, no thanks."[83] Unlike team owner Dan Snyder, who faced financial pressure from NFL sponsors for the first time in his career, the school board members found no reason to jettison their practice of using a Native American mascot.

Transcending identity politics and promoting a vision of cultural understanding requires a recognition that identities are grounded in social locations. As the philosopher Linda Alcoff reveals, "the effect of speaking for ourselves often entails the silencing of others, the erasure of their experiences and the reinscription of power relations" in such a way that a "refusal to acknowledge the importance of the differences in social identity has led to distrust, miscommunication and thus disunity."[84] Positionality can lead to radically different perspectives on whether statements such as "Make America Great Again" can be considered not only core political speech but also as a deliberate act of intimidation. Alcoff maintains that "a speaker's location (. . . her social location and social identity) has an epistemically significant impact on that speaker's claims and can serve to authorize or dis-authorize one's speech."[85]

Even among those who share an identity that serves as the basis of an organizing movement, there can be fragmentation, as when we hear some Black protestors exclaim that Black police officers relinquish their identity once they put on a blue uniform, or that a dean or president ceases to be Black when they become a part of what is deemed a monolithic administrative structure that serves to re-create systems of oppression. Voices emanating from those with privilege involving race, class, gender, and sexual orientation are often treated as "authenticating presences that confer legitimacy and credibility on the demands of subjugated speakers in a way that fails to disrupt the discursive hierarchies that operate in public spaces."[86] As a result, scholars such as E. Patrick Johnson have taken up the complex question of how one authorizes all voices in and beyond the classroom by negotiating a representation of the other "in a self-reflexive, dialogic, nonhomophobic, non-classist way."[87]

THE ROLE OF LIBERAL EDUCATION IN SPEAKING ACROSS DIFFERENCES

As a philosopher, I find these challenges and the debates over freedom of expression interesting in and of themselves. Yet, they take on particular significance for me as the president of an association whose mission it is to advance the vitality and public standing of liberal education by making equity and quality the foundation for excellence in undergraduate education in service to democracy. The very notion of a liberal education was founded on the premise that to be effective in the pursuit of truth, students' minds must be "liberated" from the habits of routinized thinking. Encouraging students to develop agency in thought, speech, and action, a liberal education, at its best, serves as an accelerator for the emergence of a cacophony of student voices and for the development of critical listening skills that invite the broadest possible range of perspectives to engage in more speech, not less.[88]

However, freedom of expression on college and university campuses must be considered not only in the abstract but also in the context of institutional mission. One of American higher education's most significant strengths is the diversity of institutions represented. Despite this diversity, the purpose of every college or university is to educate students, advance knowledge, and conduct research and scholarship in the pursuit of truth. In preparing the next generation of informed citizens who will shape our democracy, colleges and universities must remain free from entrenched and intellectually rigid forms of political partisanship and engage students from across the political spectrum. In fact, the honest and genuine pursuit of truth, at the core of a liberal education, requires tolerance for ambiguity and respect for those bearing radically different perspectives. As members of college and university communities come together and appeal to their institutional values in guiding the determination of whether speech is protected, a commitment to respect for others, free inquiry, and inclusivity must be paramount in maintaining an environment in which the free exchange of ideas can thrive.[89]

Liberal education must reflect a commitment to intellectual diversity and protection against the suppression of unpopular viewpoints as a means of guarding against political indoctrination. Insofar as colleges and universities are sites for encountering divergent perspectives, assessing conflicting ideas, evaluating competing claims of truth, creating new knowledge, and upholding intellectual integrity, a liberal education is designed to develop students' capacities to think critically and to make themselves vulnerable to criticism by welcoming dissenting voices.

Faculty members should offer curricula that includes a diversity of intellectual perspectives appropriate to their disciplines, and they must also be aware of the extent to which their positionality, framing of issues, and syllabi, together with written policies, campus cultures, and comments by other members of the community, can serve as inhibitors of speech.[90] Still, this does not mean that all ideas hold equal weight or are open for debate. Baer emphasizes this point by quoting Hannah Arendt, who wrote in 1967 that "Freedom of opinion is a farce unless factual information is guaranteed and the facts themselves are not in dispute."[91]

Further, by listening critically, one can also come to understand that not all utterances should be responded to as if they are inviting discourse. They may be assertions of belief based in reason, or they may alternatively constitute emotive expressions of trauma and suffering. Recognizing this, philosopher Mark Kingwell maintains that civil discourse is not always the appropriate response, admitting, "Sometimes you have to shout to be heard." However, he also acknowledges that "feelings cannot, by themselves, address the legacies of oppression.... Sooner or later, you have to argue."[92]

This is where a liberal education is paramount because it provides our students with the skills necessary to critically examine their assumptions and articulate a defense of their views to those who need convincing. It enables our students to discern that the way in which messages are interpreted on college and university campuses, whether contained in cartoons, email messages involving Halloween costumes, protest chants, or calls for civility, is itself a political act worthy of interrogation. But liberal education plays another role, as well, in fostering the dispositions necessary to move forward with an agreed-upon starting point in the face of an ostensibly insurmountable impasse. John Churchill, the ninth secretary of the Phi Beta Kappa Society, argued: "The best and toughest work comes when disagreement arrives at the point where what one party admits as decisive evidence for some momentous conclusion, the other party deems insufficient, or even irrelevant. That's the point we come up against when we can't see how people apparently as fully human as we are could possibly accept the reasons they do for the conclusions they reach."[93]

What is required for arriving at points of merger is engaging in sympathetic imagination—not merely the willingness to undertake a genuine consideration of how others might draw radically different conclusions from the same set of facts but also a willingness to consider the possibility that some of one's own most fundamentally held beliefs might actually be mistaken. As philosopher Martha Nussbaum observes, "Citizens cannot relate well to the complex world around them by factual knowledge alone," and moral judgment involves sympathetic participation with those who must endure the consequences of our acts.[94] When sympathetic imagination is exercised, it is much more difficult to dehumanize individuals and treat them as being outside of one's moral universe. Therefore, teaching sympathetic imagination and intellectual synthesis, which entails an identification of commonality, alongside critical thinking and effective communication, is more important than ever in a globally interdependent world and on college campuses committed to inclusive excellence and not mere diversity.

To accomplish this task, we need to enhance collaboration and integration of academic and student affairs, leveraging movements on our campuses and engaging with those in underserved communities beyond our gates. Several of the leaders of the 1998 student protests at URI are still in touch with me, and I have been struck by how many of them cite their protest experience as preparing them for leadership in their communities, in life, and in their professions. As we look ahead, knowing that there will continue to be demonstrations, demands, and debates, we should seek opportunities to encourage and guide our students in their activism, connecting the curriculum and co-curriculum through community-based learning and other high-impact practices.

Gone are the days of higher education taking place within the ivory tower—a pastoral retreat and willful disconnect from the practical matters of everyday life. If we fail to help our students connect their education to broader societal issues in ways that inspire them to lead change in a society still challenged by profound inequities, we abnegate our responsibilities to promote engaged citizenship, cultural empathy, pluralism, and diversity as the foundation for our nation's historic mission of educating for democracy.

3

PREPARING STUDENTS FOR WORK, CITIZENSHIP, AND LIFE IN THE TWENTY-FIRST-CENTURY

Reestablishing Liberal Education as a Public Good

THE GROWING ECONOMIC AND RACIAL SEGREGATION IN HIGHER EDUCATION

When the American Association of Colleges and Universities convened its 2020 annual meeting on the Future of Higher Education at the end of January in Washington, D.C., no one could have anticipated that the world as we knew it would be upended; that COVID-19, social distancing, shelter-in-place, Zoombombing, and local and national lockdowns would become part of our daily lexicon; or that a global pandemic would spur an economic recession, igniting even greater uncertainty. While colleges and universities across the country demonstrated remarkable resilience in the transition to online and remote learning, in the process, heightened awareness was brought to the food and shelter insecurities experienced by students at all types of institutions. The expansiveness of the digital divide was simultaneously unveiled as students without access to computers and high-speed internet, or who struggled with limited data plans, began lining up for college-supplied electronic devices and filling digital parking lots designed to facilitate course delivery.

In the five months that followed the initial mid-March closure of campuses, more than fifty-one million Americans filed for unemployment benefits due to job losses, exacerbating the already tenuous status of low-income students. And though the demand for higher education traditionally increases during economic recessions, a whirlwind of surveys revealed daunting statistics. Of students surveyed, four out of five reported facing significant disruption from both increased financial pressures and the need to balance work and school. Among these, approximately 40 percent said they were either "less likely" or "significantly less likely" to reenroll in college.[1] The greatest impact was on those attending community colleges, and as it turns out, enrollments at these college saw declines of up to 30 percent in the fall. This was true regardless of whether the courses were offered online.[2] Nevertheless, the effect extended to four-year institutions as well, with one study showing that of the 40 percent of aspiring first-year students "likely" or "highly likely" not to attend any four-year college, 28 percent were minoritized students and 16 percent were White.[3]

At a time when paying for college is harder than ever and students are more likely to shoulder debt burdens upon leaving, these statistics portend a less socioeconomically and racially diverse student body. Indeed, with federal financial aid covering a smaller percentage of college costs, low-income, first-generation students are encountering increasingly high barriers to college access and completion.[4] For the past three decades, much of the focus on equity in higher education has been solely on getting low-income students, especially those who are the first in their families to attend college, through the gates. However, the narrowness of this approach is highlighted by the fact that even though the percentage of students from the lowest socioeconomic quartile has risen from 32 percent in 1990 to 51 percent today, for every one hundred students from this group entering college, only twenty-one will earn a bachelor's degree within six years.

Redressing the growing economic and racial segregation in the academy is higher education's most serious challenge and will necessitate a collective call to action and a determined effort to rally the academic community in responding to the current public and political discourse that tends to isolate and privilege short-term economic benefit and promote illiberal forms of education—undermining higher education's broader civic, democratic, and cultural aims; reducing sharply the expectations of students and other stakeholders; and threatening to reproduce socioeconomic stratification.[5] Therefore, creating an ascendant narrative that contests accusations of irrelevancy and illegitimacy leveled against higher education in general and liberal education in particular is more urgent than ever.

THE ABANDONMENT OF HIGHER EDUCATION AS A PUBLIC GOOD

For those of us who believe that higher education is inextricably linked to our nation's historic mission of educating for democracy, this urgency is enhanced by the reality that we are living in an ostensibly post-truth era, characterized by the denial of authoritative knowledge and the disdain of experts, and in which rational inquiry built on evidence has all but been abandoned. Arising from an entire industry designed to sway public opinion, a rhetoric-for-hire has emerged in which the art of persuasion has been replaced by incivility and misinformation, giving rise to widespread anti-intellectualism. In this arena, asserted claims become orthodoxy regardless of the absence of evidence and in the face of enduring questions. This trend signals the extent to which the marketplace of ideas is at risk of falling prey to those who have the resources to control the shaping of public opinion and policies.

American higher education has been the victim of a false-crisis narrative, bolstered by a climate of mistrust of intellectuals and experts;

college admission scandals such as Varsity Blues, in which wealthy parents paid to have their children's test scores changed; and high-profile, red-herring cases involving freedom of expression. The consequence has been a rapid decline in public confidence in the academy. According to an annual poll conducted by Gallup, the percentage of Americans who had "a great deal" or "quite a lot of confidence" in higher education fell from 57 percent in 2015 to 48 percent in 2018, signaling the most precipitous drop in confidence experienced by any of the institutions measured, including the military, small business, police, Congress, newspapers, and labor unions.[6]

Findings from a Pew Research Center survey on Americans' views of national institutions showed similar results. In 2015, 54 percent of Republicans and 72 percent of Democrats who were polled said that colleges were having a positive influence on the country. Two years later, the same poll indicated that, for the first time since 2010, when the question began being asked, the majority of Republicans and Republican-leaning individuals, 58 percent, were convinced not only that higher education no longer has a positive impact on our society, but that it has a negative influence. By contrast, 72 percent of Democrats and Democratic-leaning respondents still viewed colleges as having a positive effect on our nation.[7]

Within a year, the partisan divide had closed, yet not in the way those of us in higher education had hoped. By 2018, 61 percent of Americans, Democrats and Republicans alike, maintained that higher education was headed in the wrong direction. Concerns ranged from the high costs of college and the belief that campuses are bastions of liberal progressivism, filled with faculty who are brainwashing a generation of snowflakes who melt at the slightest abrasion of their sensibilities, to the belief that institutions of higher education are failing to provide students with twenty-first-century skills.[8]

Perhaps the most jarring result in this series of studies was from a Gallup poll released in December 2019 showing that only 51 percent of U.S. adults now consider a college education to be very important, down from 70 percent in 2013, with younger adults, between the ages of eighteen and twenty-nine, more likely than those from other age groups to question the value of a college degree. Although the college wage premium has flattened recently, college graduates can still expect to earn over 80 percent more than those with only high school diplomas. Moreover, a college degree contributes to improved health outcomes and personal well-being, greater job security and satisfaction, increased career and networking opportunities, and more robust health insurance and retirement accounts. Nevertheless, in the minds of many, there has been a decoupling of higher education from the American dream.[9]

The growing skepticism around higher education has been fueled by politicians who have gone so far as to advocate for their state workforce needs by proposing legislation that would base funding for public colleges and universities exclusively on job acquisition for college graduates or stripping out so-called frills, such as "the search for truth," "public service," and "improving the human condition" from their university system's mission statements. In many instances, their assault on higher education targets the arts, humanities, and social sciences. As a philosopher whose father spent most of his life working as a welder, I was particularly interested in Florida senator Marco Rubio's attack on liberal education a few years ago using the dictum that we need more welders and fewer philosophers. Senator Rubio has since recanted, realizing after reading the Stoics that we need both welders and philosophers in society. Even so, he was just one voice of many in a chorus of leaders denouncing liberal education.

Rubio's Senate colleague, Rick Scott, had already laid the groundwork when serving as Florida's governor by asking: "Is it a vital interest of the state to have more anthropologists? We don't need a lot more anthropologists in the state," adding: "It's a great degree if people want to get it, but we don't need them here. I want to spend our dollars giving people science, technology, engineering, and math degrees. That's what our kids need to focus all their time and attention on, those types of degrees, so when they get out of school, they can get a job."[10]

Echoing Governor Scott's sentiments, only a few weeks after taking office, North Carolina's former governor Patrick McCrory asked his staff to write legislation that would change state funding formulas for public institutions of higher education from the number of students enrolled to the number of graduates who get jobs. McCrory commented, "It's not based on butts in seats but on how many of those butts can get jobs." He went on to challenge the value of public support for liberal arts majors, insisting: "If you want to take gender studies that's fine, go to a private school and take it. But I don't want to subsidize that if it's not going to get someone a job."[11]

For similar reasons, Sam Clovis, President Trump's educational policy advisor during the 2016 presidential campaign, announced a plan that would deny federal student loans to liberal arts majors at non-elite institutions.[12] And though he tried to redeem himself by tweeting that he was a politics and English major and learned a lot more from reading novels than textbooks, President Obama also got himself into hot water by proclaiming that "folks can make a lot more, potentially, with skilled manufacturing or the trades than they might with an art history degree."[13]

These comments each position a liberal arts education as reserved for those within the ivory tower, reflecting a willful disconnect from the practical matters of everyday life. In so doing, they foster the image of a liberal education as a self-indulgent luxury—an image that has led to the excising of humanities programs, especially in public institutions, in favor of vocational and preprofessional programs that are regarded as singularly responding to demands for economic opportunity. Talk of investing in society through education has been replaced by talk of a return on investment—tuition in exchange for jobs. The narrow focus on earning power undoubtedly makes it is easier for state legislatures and taxpayers to justify defunding higher education.

The reduction of the American dream solely to prosperity, as disconnected from the values of democracy and freedom, has contributed to the abandonment of the notion of higher education as a public good. Instead, education is viewed as a private commodity, with colleges and universities situated as sites of exclusion. Understanding the psychological factors at play in this transition, after winning the Nevada caucus during his first presidential run, Donald Trump, despite his Ivy League education, exclaimed: "I love the poorly educated! We're the smartest people, we're the most loyal people!"[14] President Trump was not only privileging hard work and common sense above intellectualism; he was also contributing to a new permission structure that supports anti-expert populism and challenges higher education's public purpose.

The public purpose of higher education is something I am particularly passionate about, not only because of my role as president of an organization whose mission it is to advance the vitality and public standing of liberal education by making quality and equity the foundations for excellence in undergraduate education in service to democracy, but also because I was the direct beneficiary of a program designed to promote civic engagement and leadership through educational opportunity. The summer I graduated from high school, I managed to escape the factory work I had done alongside my mother the previous summer only because I received funding under the federal Comprehensive Employment and Training Act (CETA). At the time, CETA funds were reserved for high school students at risk of permanent unemployment due to extreme economic and social disadvantages. That fall, I continued working thirty-five hours per week under a CETA grant, and with the additional help of Pell grants and Perkins loans, attended a local community college that had just opened in the small, rural town in which I lived. I had decided to forgo a full scholarship to my state's flagship university to serve as a caregiver for my mother, who had become chronically ill. Two years later, I transferred to Mount

Holyoke College, and within another two years was headed to Brown for my Ph.D.[15]

When I graduated, I vowed that I would never forget the lessons learned in that transition. As a result, throughout my career, I have been committed to promoting access to excellence in higher education regardless of socioeconomic background, to championing the centrality of liberal education, and to defending political scientist Benjamin Barber's notion of colleges and universities as civic missions. Barber's notion is that neither education nor research can prosper in an unfree society, and schooling, he was convinced, is society's most promising—perhaps its only—way of producing citizens who will uphold freedom.[16]

Despite continuing debates on the political stage regarding the principle of universal access to higher education as an essential symbol of equality of opportunity at the heart of the American dream, the reality is that many of our citizens still have "closed futures" and are, in a very real sense, unfree. Indeed, while the liberal-education-for-all campaign is derided by skeptics, the real danger of elitism comes from a failure to recognize the disparate impact of such rhetoric on those who are already the most marginalized and underserved members of society. The notion that we need more welders and fewer philosophers, that we should train more engineers than art historians, more people in business and industry than in anthropology, and that only those at prestigious institutions should be able to take out loans to study religion, gender studies, or the classics runs the risk of enhancing inequity by perpetuating what Thomas Jefferson referred to as an unnatural aristocracy. For this reason, we need to be vigilant in rebutting charges leveled against the liberal arts and sciences and to recognize those charges for what they are: collusion in the growth of an intellectual oligarchy in which only the very richest and most prestigious institutions preserve access to the liberal arts traditions.[17]

In these days of mounting doubt regarding the value-added of a college education, I am concerned that we are eroding democratic access to the more substantive avenues by which learning enriches us all. We are impeding access not only to the public purpose of higher education, but access to its personal purpose as well. By the personal purpose of higher education, I mean engendering the capacity to grapple with and respond to the most fundamental questions of human existence. Among the courses I signed up for during my first semester of college was an American literature class. There were not many students in that class: most enrolled in courses that more easily translated into better jobs—or any job at all. One evening my professor arranged for us to see a Hartford performance of *All the Way Home*, a Pulitzer Prize–winning play by Tad Mosel. I had never attended a professional production before, and Hartford was a world away—known only to me as the place my father traveled nightly on a third-shift bus to work at Pratt and Whitney. I remember piling into a car with my classmates, dressed in a blue velveteen jumpsuit (it was the 1970s, after all). And when the lights dimmed, I was transported. In the dark, perhaps especially in the dark, I felt part of something important. Surrounded by classmates, I stared ahead at the stage and waited for what I could not yet see.

After the play, our class went out for Chinese food and talked. The performance had raised so many big questions about faith, grief, and trust. We discussed the last act, when a wife mourns her husband's unexpected death. "I hope he loved being," she said, recognizing the possibility that he had never realized his own strength and potential. What that evening taught me, and why I remember it after all these years, is that we all have a right to experience "being." We are all entitled to live in our strength. We all deserve opportunities to find our best and most authentic selves.[18] A liberal education can be a guide to such personal enrichment, but when we imply that the only outcome disenfranchised students care about is money, we run the risk of circumscribing their futures, both personally and in the public domain. Indeed, positing employability as the lone metric for determining higher education's value precludes a consideration of the ways in which the illumination of human consciousness through literature, philosophy, music, and the arts allows us to flourish fully as human beings, enriching our experiences as individuals and as members of a community.

Still, when we characterize working-class frustrations as anti-intellectual without looking at the underlying concerns, we do so at our peril. Only by understanding the way Americans think and feel about their own economic security will we be able to comprehend the attack on colleges and universities.[19] Scholars of the White working class offer compelling insights into the mind-set of those who reject higher education at the seeming expense of their own best interest. Among these is Sherry Linkon from Georgetown University, who reminds us of the long-term benefits industrial work provided, such as allowing "workers to buy homes, send their children to college, develop work-based social networks, and enjoy stable family and community lives."[20] Comparing the toxic effects of deindustrialization to those of radioactive waste, she maintains, "If we want to understand the half-life of deindustrialization, we should listen to the stories of those who still feel the loss of economic security but also of social networks and individual possibility."[21]

Likewise, Michelle Tokarczyk, a professor at Goucher College who studies the White working class, provides a lens for understanding the disillusionment with higher education as an essential component of the American dream. For Tokarczyk, the cynicism can be traced back to the White working class's "economic anxieties and political resentments, but also their cultural fears, including their concerns about the costs of elusive upward mobility."[22] Paying the price of a college education can equate to more than tuition and loans for poor students. It can also mean bearing the cost of splintered relationships with family, friends, and community, while confronting the prospect of a loss of identity.[23]

This was certainly my experience—one I was reminded of while boarding a plane to deliver an address at a Liberal Arts Illuminated conference in Minnesota a few years ago. Just as I was about to turn my phone to airplane mode, I received an email from a Mount Holy-oke alumna who was upset that the *Boulder Daily Camera* had printed a letter to the editor that quoted me out of context. The letter was in response to an article written by a reporter who had interviewed me about the University of Colorado Board of Regents considering a proposal that would eliminate the words "liberal education" from the university's mission statement. At the end of the interview, the reporter asked, "What could a liberal education possibly do for someone study-ing medicine, law, or engineering?" As an ethicist, I talked about the ways in which technological advancements often precede thoughtful reflection about the ethical, legal, and social implications of the use of technology, especially around end-of-life issues, at times undermining patients' final wishes; about issues of environmental racism and whis-tleblowing in the context of engineering; and about how lawyers must come face-to-face with the question of the extent to which society's failure to protect people from preventable harm mitigates when the victimized become the victimizers.

Here is how what I said was interpreted by the author of the letter:

Last week the Daily Camera published an article about CU dropping the word "liberal" from its description of the type of education it provides. The article provided yet one more example of what is really wrong with our major colleges and universities.

In the article, Lynn Pasquerella, the president of the Association of American Colleges and Universities, states "the best education that we can offer students . . . is one in which students are required to engage with real-world problems across disciplines." Anyone who has followed, even peripherally, what has happened to free speech at college campuses understands the hypocrisy embedded in that statement. Can you imagine the uproar that would ensue if colleges and universities were to take up Pasquerella's charge and required students to actually "engage with real-world problems"?

Pasquerella continues by citing a benefit of a liberal education that "integrates the sciences and the arts." As could be predicted from someone who has been pickled in the coddled atmosphere of "higher" education for her entire professional life, Pasquerella perhaps unwittingly uses an example of how four years at most colleges is an expensive exercise in avoiding reality. She explains "that a liberal education can . . . inform doctors in making decisions that involve . . . a person's right to die." Heaven forbid that a doctor would learn during their university education that perhaps religious beliefs and education might play into how they handle this question. But no need for God or religion when a good liberal education can answer every question.

The perfect example of the dream world Pasquerella lives in comes from Mount Holyoke College, where she was last president. A student there wrote that at Mount Holyoke "we are politically aware and active . . . but there are the Republicans, too." Now that is the real world.[24]

Beyond predicating a false dichotomy between a liberal education and preparation for work and life and his expressed concerns about liberalism in the academy, the writer's comments reflect a deep-seated belief that a liberal education both fails to countenance and is inconsistent with the values he holds most dear—particularly religious values. By putting the word "higher" in the phrase "higher education" in quotes, he also signals a conviction that those of us at colleges and universities stigmatize the working class.

I smiled when I read his words because they recalled conversations I had with my own family. Neither of my parents had the opportunity to graduate from high school, though they both went on to earn their GEDs. My father joined the war effort at the age of sixteen, following Pearl Harbor Day, and later served in the Korean War. When he returned, he and my mother had a small wedding ceremony at the

Annapolis Naval base. She was sixteen, and it was a time when girls were not allowed to stay in school if they were married, so my mother gave up her dream of becoming an English teacher. My parents spent their lives in factories, valued hard work, and were committed to community. We attended church every Sunday, and I tagged along with my mother as she gave blood, sang in the community choir, was a member of the bowling league at Friendly Bowl, played in the bridge club, led a troop of Brownies, went to meetings of the Daughters of Isabella, and voted—they were both registered Independents. I rode with my father, who, after working all night, volunteered daily during the summers as a bus driver, bringing children with special needs to camp at Mashamoquet State Park.

I know firsthand what it is like to do piecework and to have to make a quota to get paid at the end of the week, to find refuge in the family car because there is no place else to go, to stand in a line at a pharmacy with someone behind a counter yelling at me, "Title XIX patients over here," and to be equally familiar with two groups or cultures and yet feel at home in neither. I was convinced every time I walked across campus that I would be discovered as someone who didn't really deserve a place in the academy.

That discomfort was magnified for my parents, who always felt as if they were trespassers on college campuses, no matter what the circumstances. My mother was too ill to attend my graduation from Brown, and when I invited my father, he declined, saying: "First of all, I am not going to spend over a dollar a gallon to go up that hill in Providence. And second, don't you think this makes you better than me, because it doesn't." A simple "congratulations" would have been fine, but I realized then, as I do now, the anxiety born of class structures in the United States and the real fear that arises in some families, as in my own, from imagining that the education of their children will result in a destabilizing of family unity and shared values.

Rising inequalities of wealth, income, and access to affordable college opportunities have accelerated the sowing of doubts about the value of higher education, blurring the reality that colleges and universities continue to represent powerful institutional forces in catalyzing individual and societal transformation. Now, more than ever, those of us in academia need to examine the ways in which the language of and assumptions about diversity, equity, and inclusion reinscribe college and university campuses as sites of exclusion by privileging those with social and cultural capital. The philosopher Amy Olberding reinforces this need in her superb essay "The Outsider," in which she straightforwardly rejects the cultural construct of the impostor syndrome and the price exacted for overcoming it:

> Lately, academia has grown more sensitive to how its culture flattens or normalizes those who populate its ranks. Imposter syndrome is a way of normalizing how non-standard identities can provoke alienation. Class is one such structure of exclusion, alongside race, gender, sexual identity and disability. But what are the "epistemic" costs of fitting? If we only look at alienation, we ignore the ways in which that subtly enforced sameness diminishes understanding.
>
> Academia has long been reserved for the upper class—for those with financial and, especially, cultural capital—and this limits what academics typically see or, more accurately, admit to seeing. Even though many of us do not belong to the normalized, cultured class of the stereotype, our modes of interaction often encourage us to talk as if we do. . . . The result is that the world we assay looks cleaner, simpler and more pristine than it really is.[25]

In the end, she confesses that some of her own dissatisfaction with belonging results from a "restless critical impulse, a desire to see what cleanliness is obscuring."[26]

Moreover, as philosopher Michael Sandel notes in his book *The Tyranny of Merit: What's Happened to the Common Good?*, those modes of interaction reflect a disdain for the less educated as the last acceptable prejudice. According to Sandel, the contemporary liberalism that has come to define the meritocratic political project is premised on the notion that "First, in a global, technological age, higher education is the key to upward mobility, material success and social esteem. Second, if everyone has an equal chance to rise, those who land on top deserve the rewards their talents bring."[27] He proffers that while this way of thinking is so familiar that it seems to constitute the meaning of the American dream, it has a dark side. Pointing to the implicit insult in "the idea that a college degree is a precondition for dignified work and social esteem," Sandel argues that the rhetoric of rising through educational achievement "devalues the contributions of those without a diploma, fuels prejudice against less-educated members of society, effectively excludes most people from elective government and provokes political backlash."[28]

According to Sandel, "the relentless credentialism of our days has driven working-class voters toward populist and nationalist parties and deepened the divide between those with and those without a university degree. It has also led to increasingly partisan views of higher education, the institution most emblematic of the meritocratic project."[29] The weaponization of college credentials, he writes, shows how merit can become a kind of tyranny, in which people are invited to blame those, including themselves, for not having a college degree instead of challenging inequities of wealth and esteem that are defended in the name of merit. Therefore, Sandel calls upon us to reconsider the meaning of success and question our own meritocratic hubris, positioning humility as the civic virtue most needed right now.

I was able to sit down at the kitchen table with my father and allay his fears. But, taking Sandel's cue, we need to ask what these table conversations would sound like today at the national level.

LIBERAL EDUCATION AND
THE FUTURE OF WORK

To restore public trust in higher education and destabilize the cultural attitudes at the basis of proposals that both devalue liberal education and those who have rejected it, we need to reframe the narrative, highlighting the fact that in the global knowledge economy, employer demand for graduates with a liberal education is growing. At the same time, those of us in the academy need to take seriously the underlying concerns of our most ardent critics—that higher education is too expensive, too difficult to access, and doesn't teach people twenty-first-century skills—which belie the notion Sandel forefronts, namely that "if you did not go to college, and if you are not flourishing in the new economy, your failure must be your own fault."[30]

This was part of the impetus behind AAC&U's 2018 employer research "Fulfilling the American Dream: Liberal Education and the Future of Work." The survey, conducted on behalf of AAC&U by Hart Research Associates, included the perspectives of both business executives and hiring managers, with the goal of assessing the extent to which each group believes that a college education is important and worthwhile, identifying the learning outcomes they believe are most important for success in today's economy, and discerning how prepared these different audiences perceive recent college graduates to be in these areas.

The 501 business executives at private-sector and nonprofit organizations and 500 hiring managers, whose current job responsibilities include recruiting, interviewing, and hiring new employees, express higher satisfaction with colleges and universities than the American public does as a whole. Sixty-three percent noted having either "a lot of confidence" or "a great deal of confidence" in American higher education. Business executives and hiring managers also agree upon the value of college, maintaining it is an essential and worthwhile investment of time and money. In addition to the potential for increased earnings, both executives and hiring managers cited the benefits of the accumulation of knowledge, the development of critical and analytical skills, and the pursuit of goals as especially meaningful. However, their focus was not on what students have already learned but rather on the potential to learn new things throughout their careers.[31]

Further, consistent with findings from six earlier surveys commissioned by AAC&U as part of its ongoing Liberal Education and America's Promise (LEAP) initiative, employers overwhelmingly endorse broad learning and cross-cutting skills as the best preparation for long-term career success. The college learning outcomes that executives and managers rate as most important are oral communication, critical thinking, ethical judgment, working effectively in teams, written communication, and the real-world application of skills and knowledge.[32] Internships and apprenticeships were deemed particularly valuable, with 93 percent of executives and 94 percent of hiring managers indicating that they would be more likely to hire a recent graduate who has held an internship or apprenticeship with a company or organization. Employers at nonprofits also say they are much more likely to hire recent graduates who have community-based or service-learning experience. This is predictable given that only 33 percent of executives and 30 percent of hiring managers believe that recent graduates are "very well prepared" to apply knowledge and skills in real-world settings.[33]

Colleges and universities have an obligation to educate students to become productive citizens, undoubtedly including an education that leads to financial security. Any institution that fails to incorporate ways for students to think about careers, gain workplace experience, and apply their learning is doing a disservice to those we seek to educate. For this reason, a liberal education for the twenty-first century mandates the acceleration of integrative, high-impact learning opportunities that engage every student in solving unscripted, authentic problems across all types of institutions, within the context of the workforce, not apart from it. The emphasis of the curriculum should be on learning outcomes (knowledge of human cultures and the physical and natural world, intellectual and practical skills, personal and social responsibility, integrative and applied learning) as necessary for all students' intellectual, civic, personal, and professional development and for success in a global economy. In addition, assignments should make clear the relationships among areas of knowledge. For, in a world in which rapidly changing technology means rapid obsolescence, addressing the grand challenges of the future will require the capacity for creative and integrative thinking—the type of thinking that sees academic disciplines not as separate and disconnected silos of learning but rather as varied approaches to the same enlightened end.

This conclusion was validated in a report, *The Integration of the Humanities and Arts with Sciences, Engineering, and Medicine in Higher Education: Branches from the Same Tree,* issued at the end of May 2018 by the National Academies of Sciences, Engineering, and Medicine. I served on the committee, a project of the Board of Higher Education and the Workforce, that was directed to examine whether the integration of arts and humanities with science, engineering, math, and medicine can improve learning outcomes for all students. The title of the report was taken from a quote by Albert Einstein, who in a letter written in 1937 amid the backdrop of burgeoning fascist power in central Europe, expressed consternation over "the dangerous implications of living in a society where long-established foundations of knowledge were corrupted, manipulated, and coerced by political forces."[34] Einstein maintained that "all religions, arts, and sciences are branches of the same tree."[35]

The report found the need to "achieve more effective forms of capacity building for twenty-first-century workers and citizens" through the acquisition of broad-based skills from across all disciplines "that can be flexibly deployed in different work environments across a lifetime."[36] It concludes: "In a world where science and technology are major drivers of social change, historical, ethical, aesthetic, and cultural competencies are more critical than ever. At the same time, the complex and often technical nature of contemporary issues in democratic governance demands that well-educated citizens have an appreciation of the nature of technical knowledge and of its historical, cultural, and political roles in American democracy."[37] For, "truly robust knowledge depends on the capacity to recognize the critical limitations of particular ways of knowing" and "to achieve the social relations appropriate to an inclusive and democratic society."[38]

In readying students for the future, it is crucial to understand the dangers of creating a hegemony of one tradition over others and an exaggerated trust in the efficacy of the methods of natural science applied to all areas of investigation. This was a lesson imparted nearly five decades ago when Paul Feyerabend warned against a lapse on the part of scientists into scientism in his book *Against Method*. Scientism is a doctrine according to which all genuine knowledge is scientific knowledge, reifying the scientific method as the only legitimate form of inquiry.

Despite Feyerabend's admonition, science's success in explaining the world has led to a cultural misappropriation that has conflated science with scientism. The profound societal impact of this conflation has led the astrophysicist Adam Frank to challenge defenders of scientism by calling for a clarification of how scientism manifests itself in order to "help us understand the damage it does to the real project that lies ahead of us: building space for the full spectrum of human beings in a culture fully shaped by science."[39]

Taking up Frank's charge to consider how scientism manifests itself, and especially how the metaphysics of consciousness offers the tools necessary for building the space to which he refers, we need to ask, "What would we lose, if anything, by reducing all learning and engagement to practices only rooted in the sciences?" And this is precisely the question we need to address in designing a curriculum for the twenty-first century. As Feyerabend reminds us, true scientists are not scientistic—they possess a much more nuanced and complex understanding that sensibilities cannot be granted through scientific practices. Science is a tool for investigating metaphysical and episte-mological claims. But there is also value that comes from reflecting on experiences in a manner that arouses the very sensibilities that enable us to deal with the metaphysics of being human and conscious of living in the world.

The liberal education we offer to our students is a sensibility rather than a group of subjects. Good critics of literature can bring us into a sphere of experience that combines allusions to the past with what is happening in the world right now. Like philosophers, artists, and historians, they are capable of speaking to a universality of experience, and it is unnecessary to measure how many people were illuminated to understand the impact of what they offer. Ultimately, it is this phe-nomenological engagement with the liberal arts that is incapable of being translated through scientism.[40]

As a result, the future of liberal education will require developing a deeper-level understanding across subject areas, connecting knowl-edge to experience, and adopting a holistic approach to evidence-based problem solving that incorporates diverse, sometimes contradictory points of view. The ability to engage in and learn from experiences dif-ferent from one's own and to understand how one's place in the world both informs and limits one's knowledge is essential to the key capacity to understand the interrelationships between multiple perspectives. Nowhere has the necessity for these skills been more evident than in the global response to COVID-19.

LIBERAL EDUCATION AND DEMOCRACY

In the United States, individual decision-making by those on the front lines of the fight against COVID-19 has taken place within the context of an increasingly fractured society. Consider, for instance, the debates over whether, or how quickly, states should reopen amid the pandemic. Just as the media began reporting bur-geoning evidence of the disparately negative impact of COVID-19 on communities of color—foregrounding persistent structural inequities in healthcare, income, wealth, education, access to government resources, and incarceration—organized rallies broke out across the country, demonstrating against state mandated stay-at-home orders. Demonstrators in Michigan, carrying assault weapons and tactical gear, nooses, swastikas, and Confederate flags, stormed the capitol building, demanding an end to the shutdown. In Denver, healthcare workers who took to the streets in their scrubs and masks, mobilizing silent counterprotests by blocking traffic, were threatened with violence and told to "Go to China if they wanted Communism." Both sites, and gatherings throughout the United States, were populated with protestors who insisted that the coronavirus was a hoax perpetrated by those intent on destroying the economy as a means of unseating President Trump. These clashing perspectives over how much individual liberty should be sacrificed for the public good reflect the fact that partisan divides in America are greater than they have been in more than half a century, jeopardizing our democracy.

Democracy cannot flourish in a nation divided into haves and have-nots, and in this age of increasing polarization, partisanship, and post-truth rhetoric, advancing liberal education —unleashing the potential of those otherwise most likely to be excluded from full participation in civic and economic life—is critical. When the board of directors of AAC&U expanded the organization's mission in 2012 to embrace inclusive excellence as central to liberal education, the goal was to signal a commitment to the ideal that access to educational excellence for all students—not just the privileged—is essential not only for a thriving economy but, more importantly, for democracy.

Since our nation's inception, institutions of higher education were established with the goal of educating for democracy, preparing knowledgeable citizens and leaders. As a matter of fact, questions regarding how American colleges and universities can best prepare students for work, citizenship, and life are as old as the nation itself. In 1751, when Benjamin Franklin founded the College of Philadelphia, he sought a new model of education for an emerging nation. Rather than engaging students in the classical curriculum of the European elite, Franklin was convinced that an education grounded in the practical matters of everyday life and centered on the teaching of English and history would serve both students and society. Pointing to the need for innovation, democratic participation, and opportunities for social mobility in a dynamic new world, Franklin nevertheless believed that higher education's ultimate goals were service to humanity and pursuit of the public good.[41]

According to historian Jill Lepore, Franklin once wrote that he wished, rather than have an "ordinary death," he could be "immersed in a cask of Madeira wine" and brought back one hundred years later to witness what had become of the country he loved (and helped create).[42] If we could invite Franklin into our living rooms today, it would likely come as no surprise to him that it was Samwell Tarly, the clumsy intellectual, who proposes democracy when members of the Great Council are charged with determining the future of the Seven Kingdoms in the finale of the HBO blockbuster *The Game of Thrones*. Tarly's fellow council members engage in a swift, wholesale repudiation of establishing a democracy and letting all the inhabitants choose the next leader of Westeros, devolving into laughter at the mere suggestion. One offers the rejoinder, "Maybe we should give the dogs a vote as well."

Dubiousness regarding the wisdom of democracy has long been a topic of philosophical treatises, from Plato's *Republic* to Ronald Dworkin's *Is Democracy Possible Here? Principles for a New Political Debate*. Dworkin's contemporary discourse confronts a pointed challenge for democracies during periods of extreme polarization, when partisan divides reach the point where we are no longer partners in self-government, and "our politics are rather a form of war." He warns: "Democracy can be healthy with no serious political argument if there is nevertheless a broad consensus about what is to be done. It can be healthy even if there is no consensus if it does have a culture of argument. But it cannot remain healthy with deep and bitter divisions and no real argument, because it then becomes only a tyranny of numbers."[43] According to Dworkin, a true democracy requires propelling public debate, or alternatively finding common ground even in the absence of consensus.

If colleges and universities are to develop the independent and critical thinkers necessary to ensure that democracy is more than the tyranny of numbers forecast in *The Game of Thrones*, we must collectively reaffirm the role that a liberal education plays in discerning the truth; the ways in which it serves as a catalyst for interrogating the sources of narratives, including history, evidence, and facts; the ways in which a liberal education promotes an understanding that the world is a collection of interdependent yet inequitable systems; the ways in which it expands knowledge of human interactions, privilege, and stratification; and the ways in which higher education fosters equity and justice, locally and globally.[44]

It is a type of education that, by its very nature, liberates the mind to seek the truth unencumbered by dogma, ideology, or prejudice. As AAC&U fellow and former Goucher president José Bowen wrote in a 2019 end-of-the-year commentary in *The Hill*:

> Education should be about change and not just content . . . to produce self-regulated learners who can more easily change their mind in the future. This is also how democracy is supposed to work. . . . Education should prepare you for the unknown and for uncertainty, in part, by giving you some standards for your continual pursuit of new truths. Educators have always hoped to foster both a desire to seek truth and a tolerance for ambiguity. . . . Our future depends not on more certainty, but on the ability to change our minds in the face of new information, new data, and indeed, new criticism.[45]

The distinctively American tradition of liberal education is not only appropriate to democracy but essential to fostering the sustained engagement of free individuals committed to our shared values of justice, liberty, human dignity, and the equality of persons. These fundamental democratic ends are fortified by liberal education's emphasis on evidence-based reasoning, encouraging dialogue across difference, cultivating rational debate, and engendering the habits of heart and mind that both equips students and disposes them to civic involvement and the creation of a more just and inclusive society.[46]

The positing of liberal education as a valuable mechanism for advancing democracy was affirmed in a 2020 report by Anthony Carnevale and his colleagues at Georgetown's Center for Education and the Workforce. *The Role of Education in Taming Authoritarian Attitudes* examines the role of colleges and universities in relation to the challenge of rising authoritarianism at the global level and the resulting threat to democracies. The study identifies authoritarianism as a worldview that leads individuals to prefer authority and uniformity over autonomy and diversity and appeals to research developed by political psychologist Karen Stenner that measures individuals' inclinations toward either "independent thought, respect for diversity, and inquisitive assessment of evidence" or "unquestioning deference to authority."[47]

Comparing the attitudes and preferences of people from fifty-one countries, the study found that those living in the United States have moderate authoritarian preferences, ranking sixteenth worldwide, on par with Estonia, Chile, and Uruguay. Although Germany, New Zealand, Sweden, and Ghana were the countries whose residents were least likely to express authoritarian tendencies, the United States has the strongest association between being college educated and a lower propensity toward authoritarianism.

Citing the power of liberal education in mitigating against authoritarian tendencies, the study's findings unveil that college graduates at both the bachelor's-degree and associate's-degree levels are less likely to express authoritarian preferences and attitudes than those with less education. The researchers proffer that this is likely a consequence of the emphasis on vocational preparation within European models of education and training, as opposed to American higher education's focus on general education and exposure to the liberal arts. Indeed, the researchers found that liberal arts students are less inclined than those studying business or the STEM disciplines—science, technology, engineering, and math—to adopt attitudes of political intolerance, signified by the inclination toward the repression of free speech, xenophobia, nativism, racism, ethnocentrism, and religious sectarianism.[48]

The authors of the study point to the ways in which authoritarianism tends to flourish when social norms and personal security are threatened. Rising inequalities of wealth and income in the United States, the devastating impact of COVID-19, and divisions over issues of racial and social justice, including the rights of immigrants, have fueled feelings of vulnerability among many Americans, who are then more likely to seek the protection of authoritarian leaders and political systems. And when those with high authoritarian inclinations identify strongly with specific groups, a threat to those groups can result in greater intolerance and a resistance to changing one's views.[49] This is supported by studies on racial intolerance in America demonstrating that when people in majority groups feel threatened, they support military rule and government actions antithetical to democracy that would prevent people of color, immigrants, and those speaking languages other than English from moving into their neighborhoods.[50]

According to the study, liberal education reduces individuals' sensitivities to potential triggers by providing psychological protection in the form of self-esteem, personal security, and autonomy. It also fosters a level of interpersonal trust associated with lower inclinations toward expressing authoritarian attitudes and preferences. The capacity to deal with complexity and diversity and not be threatened by differences of opinion is significant given that perceptions of threat—to physical safety, economic security, group identity, social norms—often activate authoritarian tendencies. Exposure of liberal arts majors to diverse contexts, histories, ideas, lifestyles, religions, ways of life, and cultures diminishes the likelihood that differing worldviews will trigger authoritarian responses and increases the chances of their being countered with evidence. Engagement with the liberal arts also encourages empathy and tolerance.[51]

Furthermore, the findings reveal that postsecondary education leads to greater political participation and civic engagement. This, in turn, decreases tendencies toward authoritarianism, regardless of political affiliation. Because democracies with higher levels of education have greater levels of political tolerance and are more likely to survive, the report concludes that "higher education is the cornerstone of successful democracies not easily shaken by authoritarian threats."[52]

The Role of Education in Taming Authoritarian Attitudes displays the gravity of broadening access to higher education. However, making equity a pervading focus of educational reform and innovation will require colleges and universities to move beyond the goals of access and compositional diversity to conceive of and deliver the types of educational experiences, grounded in liberal education, that support the success of all students, regardless of the institutions they attend. Understanding this, Wesleyan president Michael Roth has long argued that a liberal education must couple intellectual diversity with civic education through participation.

Roth appeals to the precepts that (1) developing civic preparedness is a core element of the mission of American higher education; (2) participating in American political life helps students learn from a diversity of ideas and people, while developing skills for lifelong active citizenship; and (3) empowering students and teachers to engage with the complex issues facing the country are crucial facets of higher education's contributions to the public good.[53] A variety of institutions are leading the way in educating for democracy. Mercer University's Center for Community Engagement has made a palpable commitment to promoting civil discourse. Rutgers–Newark, Wagner College, Kingsborough Community College, and California State University–Chico have also been particularly thoughtful in how they have engaged community leaders in underserved areas and how they have supported a diversity of community-engaged experiences, including town hall events and public debates that expose students to what it means to connect learning with civic issues and dialogue across difference.

INCLUSIVE EXCELLENCE

However, the approach to liberal education that has been outlined contests the continued primacy of now outmoded curricular designs and institutional structures, including distribution models of general education that privilege departmental structures and promote disciplinary silos at the expense of integrative, applied, and community-based learning. Writing for AAC&U on her book *The New Education,* the Ness Award–winner and higher-education scholar Cathy Davidson elucidates the ways in which so much of higher education today is a product of factory models designed for efficiency 150 years ago.

According to Davidson: "The great project of the nineteenth century was to train farmers to be factory workers and to turn shopkeepers into a professional managerial class. Everyone from Karl Marx to Adam Smith talked about how formal, compulsory schooling was designed to train children to time, task, duty, hierarchy, and authority. This is one reason the school bell became the century's symbol of public education."[54] She notes that as the modern American research university arose between 1860 and 1925, "a range of systems and structures for regularizing, specializing, and measuring learning became fully institutionalized, . . . including majors, minors, electives, graduate and professional schools, degree requirements, credit hours, grades, multiple-choice tests, college entrance exams, tenure, sabbaticals, faculty pensions, school rankings, donor-named chairs, corporate-sponsored research, failure, and more."[55]

Acknowledging the extent to which our majors and minors are designed to replicate the specialized training of the professoriate, as opposed to responding to the needs of the contemporary world, Davidson seeks a new Copernican revolution in the way we think about the purpose of higher education—one that will disrupt the current systems and structures no longer serving the needs of twenty-first-century students. In addition to breaking down the barriers impeding integrative, problem-based learning designed to address problems that matter to the student and to society, this revolution must also include a transition away from an expert model in which students are passive recipients of knowledge to one in which liberal learners actively engage with knowledge, participating in its creation and expansion.

A focus on inclusive excellence empowers liberal learners to appropriate the knowledge and skills represented by essential learning outcomes to make them their own. This, consequently, requires embracing a paradigm shift from ranking and sorting students to ensuring that all students benefit from the most powerful forms of learning. Student success depends not on the "college readiness" of individual students but rather on the readiness of the institution to welcome and support all students and to respond to the changing needs of an increasingly diverse society. Reconceived as a process rather than an outcome, excellence in higher education entails providing students with regular opportunities to demonstrate achievement in a range of knowledge and skills areas across their educational experiences and pathways. In addition, it requires assessing students in ways that promote continuous improvement.[56] The embrace of inclusive excellence as a process has evolved from, and builds upon, the earlier shift in higher education from instruction to learning and focuses on faculty-driven innovation related to active and applied forms of problem-centered, inquiry-based learning and the exploration of a significant problem that is defined personally by each student. This type of "signature work" centers on student initiatives, interests, and insights, encompassing cumulative learning and high-impact practices.

For far too long, educators have relied on assessments that ask students questions for which we already know the answers. Preparing students for the unscripted problems of the future will necessitate jettisoning standardized tests and developing more equitable forms of assessment. There has been some progress toward this end emerging as a result of the impact of COVID-19 on higher education. The need for social distancing to prevent the spread of the coronavirus caused SAT and ACT testing centers to shut down. This led to a flurry of top-ranked national liberal arts colleges and universities, including Harvard, Brown, Cornell, Amherst, and Williams, waiving their standardized test requirements for the fall of 2021 and beyond.

The College Board's announcement that they were developing an online test that students could take at home raised an outcry over issues of equity. These compounded existing concerns over issues of discrimination based on race, class, gender, and disability status related to testing. In fact, increased attention to the lack of availability of expensive test preparation; stereotype threat, which raises self-doubt and increases anxiety for those who are negatively stereotyped; and the myth of meritocracy revealed by the Varsity Blues scandal resulted in a lawsuit being filed against the University of California system.[57] The plaintiffs called for the elimination of the SAT or ACT requirement, claiming the tests are biased and not an accurate predictor of academic success. The trend toward more equitable assessment in the admission process and throughout a student's education carries potential for contributing positively to completion rates of low-income students, especially at elite institutions, and to their social mobility.

Quality assessment entails the evaluation of applied learning experiences, directed at student agency. Rather than standardized tests, the most promising assessment approach evaluates samples of authentic student work using scoring guides, or rubrics that are keyed to essential learning outcomes. Rubric-based assessment across diverse learning pathways provides a window on the development and application of skills over time, as opposed to how a student performs on a single exam or assignment. Assessment of liberal education, at its best, is based on a demonstration of proficiencies regarding complex interrelated problems that draw upon multiple disciplinary and experiential lenses, while evaluating dimensions of students' formation as global citizens and problem solvers.

Moreover, assignments should make clear their learning objectives and be scaffolded in a way that moves toward engaging students in increasingly complex work. This approach is a critical step in encouraging students to reflect on how the academic work they are doing today is creating capacities that will serve them tomorrow in their employment and as citizens. As Jeff Selingo points out in his book *There Is Life after College,* students who are most successful upon graduation are those who can create a compelling narrative about the connections between their curriculum and their career aspirations. Yet, only about one-third of the 752 young people Selingo surveyed for his book could do so. Unlike these so-called "sprinters," a majority of students are either "wanderers" or "stragglers." Such students have ill-defined trajectories, are apt to start but not finish college, or may take six or eight years to complete, without any real idea of how their degree connects to their specific career objectives.

There are distinctive class markers in the categories of students that Selingo outlines. Students who cannot afford to take internships and must take jobs unrelated to their career goals so that they can pay off student debt will have a more difficult time than those without college-loan burdens and who have had at least one internship. Yet, even among the latter group, without guidance from professors, the connection between a liberal education and their professional aspirations can be elusive for students, causing them to question the value of their degree. My son Pierce was one of these undergraduates. He started college wanting to go into television and film production and railed against what he saw as the hoops he had to jump through just to get behind a camera. One day, he walked into the library of the president's house at Mount Holyoke to find me writing a paper; his father, who is an entomologist, studying a text; and his twin brother, Spencer, working toward his Ph.D. in African American studies. Looking out the window on a perfect October day, he uttered in disgust, "This is the most dysfunctional family on the planet."

When I asked him to expand on his observation, Pierce announced that we should "be out in the world doing things." I reminded him that intellectual pursuits were in fact things in the world and that he might have his own studies to engage in. He replied by saying that the courses left in his curriculum had no bearing on what he would be doing in life: "They are just trying to get our money by making me take courses that I will never use, like Small Group Communication and Intercultural Competence."

As luck would have it, Pierce's first job in graduate school was working for NBC Universal on the *Jerry Springer Show*, where he came to understand that we were not, in fact, the *most* dysfunctional family on the planet. One day he called excitedly to say, "Guess what? I booked the talent today." When I explained why he might want to use a different phrase to describe his work, he admitted the real reason he was calling. "Okay," he said, "now I understand the value of a liberal education. I had to run out and get ties and cigarettes for the talent and spend two hours in the green room with them. I finally get why I needed to take courses in small group communication and intercultural competence."

If we are to meaningfully address the completion problem in American higher education, we must do a better job helping all students draw these types of linkages in each of their classes, making explicit why we are asking them to engage with certain material and to perform specific tasks. This work becomes all the more critical at a time when students and parents are increasingly skeptical about whether a liberal education is worth the price. My son was not at risk of dropping out of college due to the cost of courses that at the time he considered irrelevant. Yet, for many, the lack of understanding over the significance of the curriculum will mean the difference between completing a degree and dropping out.

Technology has provided enhanced tools, such as ePortfolios, for helping students make sense of their cumulative experience, while making it possible to see and to demonstrate to others that their liberal education is worth more than the sum of its parts. Their use allows us to account for the fact that learning is not confined to the classroom and that it occurs within and across a range of curricular, cocurricular, and extracurricular experiences. Promoting reflection on assignments through ePortfolios facilitates meaning making in ways that help students monitor individual progress, understand why they are being asked to do what the curriculum requires of them, and apply their learning in other contexts and settings. In addition, it contributes to the creation of a powerful personal narrative by students that connects curriculum to career in ways that Selingo illustrates have a profound impact on the trajectory of their careers.

Finally, assessment practices that emphasize the learning process and outcomes can reduce stress for students who are worried about failing or who lack the social and cultural capital needed to understand that they deserve a place in the academy. If we are to fulfill the promise of American higher education and ensure that all students are benefiting from educational practices that support student success, colleges and universities must be places of welcome and belonging. Cia Verschelden's compelling research highlights how stress from economic insecurities, racism, and a sense of belonging uncertainty reduce the amount of cognitive bandwidth available for learning. COVID-19 and the financial fallout from the pandemic will add further stress for many students in the coming semesters, whether they are on campus or learning remotely. Faculty, staff, and administrators must do everything possible to deepen a sense of belonging and inclusion and encourage a growth mind-set in students by offering opportunities for continuous improvement that can promote intellectual risk taking.

Belonging uncertainty among underserved students can also be reduced when colleges and universities make a commitment to serving as anchor institutions, demonstrating that their success is intertwined with the economic, educational, health, and psychosocial well-being of those in the communities in which they are located. Active engagement with diverse individuals around real-world challenges, taking advantage of local epistemologies, can create pathways for students and establish an enhanced sense of belonging crucial to individual thriving. If people who feel threatened due to economic, physical, psychological, and other insecurities are more likely to resist differing views, they will be reluctant to pursue college. Building trust and being visible within our communities can make a difference.

In fact, if we are to contest the widespread perception that colleges and universities are out of touch with the needs of society, those of us championing liberal education must use whatever modes of engagement are available to us to connect the work being done in the academy with people's lives—not just through community-based learning but through radio, television, videos, tweets, blogs, theater, hip-hop. For example, Anna Deavere Smith, founder and director of Harvard's Institute on the Arts and Civic Dialogue, uses documentary theater to demonstrate this capacity while confronting some of the most pressing social issues of the day. In her linguistic ethnography and one-woman show *Talk to Me: Listening between the Lines,* Smith places herself in "other people's words" in the way that one might place oneself in another's shoes. Her objective has been to "reignite our collective imagination about what it's like to be the 'other person'" and to "show the empathetic soul of American identities whose words wait and create change." A riff on John Cage's notion that "We only hear what listen for," Smith insists, "If there is any hope for us, it lies in relearning to tell the truth and hear it, in reclaiming ourselves as a listening space."[58] By doing so, we will prove false Mark Twain's humorous assertion that "All schools, all colleges, have two great functions: to confer, and to conceal, valuable knowledge."[59]

If academics rely exclusively on the mechanics of arcane study to get out our message, failing to utilize the most vibrant vectors for helping citizens to cope with humanistic questions, scholarly pursuits as anything more than an ossified depository of ancient curiosity will die. Relinquishing the opportunities that would extend our reach and leaving these channels of communication to the media moguls will result in the continuing decline of public discourse, while academicians lose the chance to engender a true sense of wonder purely for the sake of didacticism. Individuals will still thirst for humanistic guidance in seeking answers to their questions and compass points for their endeavors, but the academy as an institution will become nothing more than self-referential, as the frames of humanistic practice disappear forever.

Unfortunately, we are at a point in our history when the professional structures of academic scholarship, with its tendency to neglect teaching excellence, outreach, civic engagement, and public intellectualism, are alienated from a more widespread humanistic comportment to life—and thus from the very purpose of a liberal education. Until we change both the curricula and the reward systems within the academy, structural impediments will continue to marginalize the critical work of those dedicated to providing the broadest access to higher education through humanistic practice—practice that reaches beyond the gates.

Of course, the higher education landscape needs and feeds upon specialization, and I would certainly not recommend abandoning technical and intricate research as a foundation for addressing questions and fueling endeavors. But such activity should be measured in humanistic terms—not by eliminating scholarship but by broadening what we value as an expression of that mastery. And yet at present, we go so far as to discourage pretenured faculty from focusing too much on teaching and service. Activities engaging actual, questioning human beings, whether in the classroom or in the community, drop out of professional focus. Academic institutions, with the help of disciplinary societies, should actively reconsider pathways to recruitment, tenure, and promotion, placing scholarship into reasonable balance with humanistic modes of activity in the classroom and beyond.

Canadian philosopher Mark Kingwell observes that while those of us in the academy may eschew populism and its condemnation of life in the ivory tower, "we are losing when it comes to reason and critical intelligence and civility. We are losing when it comes to the basic justification of what we do. We are losing on defending universities as forces for good."[60] Kingwell argues that it is despicable to enjoy the fruits of academic success and not feel a profound sense of obligation "to demonstrate why our efforts have wider value than just our personal satisfaction." I could not agree more.

For this reason, in my inaugural message to the AAC&U community when I was appointed president, and again, when I was appointed the president of the Phi Beta Kappa Society, I referenced a letter written in May 1863 by Emily Dickinson to two of her cousins. In a nation enmeshed in the Civil War, she confessed, "I must keep 'gas' burning to light the danger up, so I could distinguish it." The poet's words reflect her unflinching pursuit of the truth, and the need she felt to move beyond her own narrow viewing point. Dickinson wanted to "light the danger up"—not turn away from it. She sought to look at what others either could not or did not want to see. In the midst of national dissension and uncertainty, she strove to use every ounce of her being in the process of discovery—perhaps understanding that deliberative democracy, especially in times of crisis, relies on the creation of a critical public culture that foments reasoned debate and independent thought.

One hundred years later, during the 1963 March on Washington, in a nation still divided, Dr. Martin Luther King Jr. said: "We are now faced with the fact that tomorrow is today. We are confronted with the fierce urgency of now. In this unfolding conundrum of life and history, there 'is' such a thing as being too late. This is no time for apathy or complacency. This is a time for vigorous and positive action."

Paying attention to the object lessons of both Dickinson and King is more critical than ever. We need to light up the danger and illuminate the transformative power of a liberal education. At the same time, we need to face the fierce urgency of now, recognizing that higher education and its graduates must play a leadership role in fulfilling the promise of liberal education for all, ensuring that every student is positioned to find their best and most authentic selves.

AFTERWORD

I got to know Dr. Lynn Pasquerella a few years ago, when we worked together on *The Integration of the Humanities and Arts with Sciences, Engineering, and Medicine in Higher Education: Branches from the Same Tree*, a consensus study report from the National Academies of Sciences, Engineering, and Medicine. I recognized then that Dr. Pasquerella and I have a lot in common: we both have been university presidents, lead academic associations, and are outspoken advocates for accessible and inclusive education that encompasses the sciences, arts, and humanities.

I have come to admire Dr. Pasquerella's work not only for her many academic accomplishments and her contributions to the *Branches from the Same Tree* report, which remains just as relevant today, but also for her lifelong dedication to students. As her career has taken her from philosophy professor to university president to president of the American Association of Colleges and Universities (AAC&U), she has remained steadfast in her objective to ensure that all students have access to excellence in liberal education, regardless of their backgrounds. Recently, she led the AAC&U in creating an institute for racial healing. The term "thought leader" may be overused, but I can think of no better descriptor for Dr. Pasquerella, as her scholarship and leadership have inspired many academic institutions to create centers of racial justice on their campuses.

Her thought leadership continues in *What We Value,* and it is a great honor to read and comment on the essays in this collection. Dr. Pasquerella's comprehensive conversations about educational disparities, behavioral health, free speech, and student safety are always pertinent—but never more than today, when long-standing issues in higher education and healthcare are exacerbated and often politicized.

I was struck by the essays' underlying contention that listening is fundamental to change, especially amid today's political echo chambers. It is often easy for many of us in academia to lean toward the political left—or to be perceived to lean that way—and to isolate ourselves from other ideologies. However, the issues of today require listening to and learning from multiple perspectives, including those with which we may disagree. This does not defend hateful, unfounded, or dangerous views, which we must vigorously oppose on campuses and in society. That said, listening to each other in respectful ways, especially when we disagree, is more important than ever. As our world continues to become more complex and diverse—and, unfortunately, more fractured—it will be critical to discuss ideas productively and seek to understand each other, regardless of our political differences.

I happen to agree with many of the ideas expressed in these essays, such as the need for physicians to discuss end-of-life care directly with patients, a situation I have faced personally as a cardiologist. Whether caring for patients or serving students, I have seen that the best way to create progress is to listen first. My career in medicine taught me that I do not have all the answers—no one does. We must engage in dialogue not only with other physicians, scientists, and academics but also with patients and their families, students, and community members. Creating space for thoughtful, productive discourse is perhaps the most important thing we can do to tackle society's greatest challenges.

The arts and humanities help us listen. They cultivate empathy, understanding, and nuance. I know this not only from my academic background and from the *Branches from the Same Tree* report I worked on with Dr. Pasquerella but also from my own lived experience. I helped finance my college education by playing the saxophone in a rhythm and blues band in Chicago, and I continue to integrate music into my life today. I am certain that my musical experiences have helped me become a better physician, educator, and leader. It is through listening—to music and to others—that I have been able to learn and grow throughout my career.

I have long believed that society's most complex issues, from poverty to racism to health inequity, require an integrated approach for this reason. We need science, but we also need each other—and the arts and humanities are the connective tissue we need to heal and thrive.

Over recent years we have seen this plainly, as it has taken more than scientific research to mitigate the COVID-19 pandemic. Science alone was not enough to face the disproportionately low vaccine distribution among marginalized communities, or to begin to quell the distrust surrounding whether to accept vaccination. These societal issues required clear communication, critical thinking, ethical judgment, and applied knowledge of social justice—all skills that the arts and humanities help teach us.

A union between the sciences, arts, and humanities is a powerful force. The arts and humanities do not compete with the STEMM (science, technology, engineering, mathematics, and medicine) fields but complement them and advance our shared objective of creating a healthier and more just world. We can only succeed in addressing the problems of today when we combine these disciplines and open our eyes, ears, and hearts to other perspectives.

This conjures a quotation from no less an academic than Albert Einstein: "All religion, arts, and sciences are branches of the same tree. All these aspirations are directed toward ennobling man's life, lifting it from the sphere of mere physical existence and leading the individual towards freedom." It was this quotation that gave the name to the *Branches from the Same Tree* report and that continues to inspire both Dr. Pasquerella and me today to lead by listening.

This collection of essays is one I will turn to again and again as I work with my colleagues at the Association of American Medical Colleges in navigating a path toward a healthier future for people everywhere. I hope that you find the same value in these essays as I do: a recommitment to listening to others and creating spaces for inclusive dialogue, whether or not we agree. This is the true value of free speech—to learn from each other.

DAVID J. SKORTON, MD

President and CEO of the Association of American Medical Colleges (AAMC)

NOTES

INTRODUCTION

1. Michael Brice-Saddler, "Memorial Held Outside White House in Solemn Reminder of More Than 200,000 Americans Killed by COVID-19," *Washington Post,* October 4, 2020.
2. Grant Schulte, "Michigan Governor Says Trump's Words Inspire Extremists," *Washington Post,* October 8, 2020.
3. Schulte, "Michigan Governor Says Trump's Words Inspire Extremists."
4. The Moral Machine Game, https://www.moralmachine.net.

1. MORAL DISTRESS, MORAL INJURY, AND THE CONCEPT OF DEATH AS UN-AMERICAN

1. Alain De Botton, "Camus on the Coronavirus," *New York Times,* March 19, 2020.
2. De Botton, "Camus on the Coronavirus."
3. American Medical Association Code of Ethics (Chicago: American Medical Association Press, 1847), 105.
4. American Medical Association Code of Ethics, June 2016, https://www.ama-assn.org/delivering-care/ethics/ama-code-medical-ethics-guidance-pandemic.

5. Ali Watkins, Michael Rothfeld, William K. Rashbaum, and Brian M. Rosenthal, "Top E.R. Doctor Who Treated Virus Patients Dies by Suicide," *New York Times*, April 27, 2020.

6. Jianbo Lai, Simeng Ma, Ying Wang, et al., "Factors Associated with Mental Health Outcomes among Health Care Workers Exposed to Coronavirus Disease 2019," *Journal of the American Medical Association*, March 23, 2020.

7. Lai, Ma, Wang, et al., "Factors Associated with Mental Health Outcomes."

8. M. C. Corley, "Nurse Moral Distress: A Proposed Theory and Research Agenda," *Nursing Ethics* 9, no. 6 (November 2002): 636–50.

9. Blake Farmer, "When Doctors Struggle with Suicide, Their Profession Often Fails Them." *Morning Edition*, NPR, July 31, 2018, audio.

10. Wendy Dean and Simon Talbot, "Moral Injury and Burnout in Medicine: A Year of Lessons Learned," *STAT*, July 26, 2019.

11. Dean and Talbot, "Moral Injury and Burnout in Medicine."

12. Dean and Talbot, "Moral Injury and Burnout in Medicine."

13. Arnold Toynbee first raised the concept of death as un-American, "an affront to every citizen's right to life, liberty, and the pursuit of happiness," in *Changing Attitudes toward Death in the Modern Western World*, ed. Toynbee et al. (New York: McGraw Hill, 1968), 131.

14. Jake Harper, "As COVID-19 Spreads, It's Time to Discuss End of Life Plan," *Side Effects: Public Health Personal Stories*, WFYI Live Radio, April 6, 2020, audio.

15. Carin Van Zyl and Dawn M. Gross, "For People Dying to Talk, It Finally Pays to Listen with Reimbursable Advance Care Planning," *AMA Journal of Ethics*, August 2018.

16. Jo Cavallo, "Using Video Support Tools to Facilitate End-of-Life Discussions with Patients: A Conversation with Angelo E. Volandes, MD, MPH," *ASCO Post*, May 10, 2018.

17. Jaclyn Portanova, Jennifer Allshire, Catherine Perez, Anna Rahman, and Susan Enguidanos, "Ethnic Difference in Advance Care Directive Completion and Care Preferences: What Has Changed in a Decade?" *Journal of the American Geriatric Society* 65, no. 6 (March 9, 2017).

18. Portanova, Allshire, Perez, Rahman, and Enguidanos, "Ethnic Difference in Advance Care Directive Completion and Care Preferences."

19. Marcella Alsan and Marianne Wanamaker, "Tuskegee and the Health of Black Men," National Bureau of Economic Research, June 2016, https://www.nber.org/papers/w22323.

20. Alsan and Wanamaker, "Tuskegee and the Health of Black Men."

21. Amanda Machado, "Why Many Latinos Dread Going to the Doctor," *The Atlantic*, May 7, 2014.

22. Machado, "Why Many Latinos Dread Going to the Doctor."

23. "COVID-19 in Racial and Ethnic Minority Groups," June 25, 2020, https://www.cdc.gov/coronavirus/2019-ncov/community/health-equity/racial-ethnic-disparities/index.html.

24. Nathan Chomilo, Nia Heard-Garris, Malini DeSilva, and Uché Blackstock, "The Harm of a Colorblind Allocation of Scarce Resources," *Health Affairs*, April 30, 2020.

25. Chomilo, Heard-Garris, DeSilva, and Blackstock, "The Harm of a Colorblind Allocation of Scarce Resources."

26. Chomilo, Heard-Garris, DeSilva, and Blackstock, "The Harm of a Colorblind Allocation of Scarce Resources."

27. Chomilo, Heard-Garris, DeSilva, and Blackstock, "The Harm of a Colorblind Allocation of Scarce Resources."

28. Chomilo, Heard-Garris, DeSilva, and Blackstock, "The Harm of a Colorblind Allocation of Scarce Resources."

29. Cavallo, "Using Video Support Tools."

30. *Arato v. Avedon,* Court of Appeal, Second District, Division 3, California, 1992, https://caselaw.findlaw.com/ca-court-of-appeal/1759004.html.

31. *Arato v. Avedon.*

32. Mary S. McCabe and Courtney Storm, "When Doctors and Patients Disagree about Medical Futility," *Journal of Oncological Practice* 4, no. 4 (July 4, 2008): 207–9.

33. Larry R. Churchill, *Ethics for Everyone: A Skills-Based Approach* (Oxford: Oxford University Press, 2019), 125–27.

34. Jerome Groopman, *The Anatomy of Hope: How People Prevail in the Face of Illness* (New York: Random House, 2005), xiv, 210.

35. Angie Drobnic Holan, "PolitiFact's Lie of the Year: 'Death Panels.'" *PolitiFact*, December 18, 2009.

36. Holan, "PolitiFact's Lie of the Year."

37. Holan, "PolitiFact's Lie of the Year."

38. Holan, "PolitiFact's Lie of the Year."

39. Holan, "PolitiFact's Lie of the Year."
40. Felicia Sonmez, "Texas Lt. Gov. Dan Patrick Comes under Fire for Saying Seniors Should 'Take a Chance' on Their Own Lives for Sake of Grandchildren during Coronavirus Crisis," *Washington Post,* March 24, 2020.
41. Alfred F. Connors, Neal V. Dawson, Norman A. Desbiens, et al., "A Controlled Trial to Improve Care for Seriously Ill Hospitalized Patients: The Study to Understand Prognoses and Preferences for Outcomes and Risks of Treatments (SUPPORT)," *Journal of the American Medical Association* 274, no. 20 (1995): 1591–98. Note that this study is distinct from a 2005 one using the same acronym, the Surfactant, Positive Pressure, and Oxygenation Randomized Trial (SUPPORT), which focused on the amount of supplemental oxygen given to extremely premature infants.
42. Connors, Dawson, Desbiens, et al., "A Controlled Trial to Improve Care for Seriously Ill Hospitalized Patients."
43. Connors, Dawson, Desbiens, et al., "A Controlled Trial to Improve Care for Seriously Ill Hospitalized Patients."
44. Connors, Dawson, Desbiens, et al., "A Controlled Trial to Improve Care for Seriously Ill Hospitalized Patients."
45. Connors, Dawson, Desbiens, et al., "A Controlled Trial to Improve Care for Seriously Ill Hospitalized Patients."
46. Robert Wood Johnson Foundation, "Before I Die," https://www.thirteen.org/bid/p-johnson.html.
47. George Annas, "How We Lie," *The Hastings Center Report,* November/December 1995, https://www.onlinelibrary.wiley.com.
48. Sherwin Nuland, *How We Die: Reflections on Life's Final Chapter* (New York: Penguin, 1994), 253.
49. Lewis M. Cohen, *No Good Deed: A Story of Medicine, Murder Accusations, and the Debate over How We Die* (New York: HarperCollins, 2010), 12.
50. Cohen, *No Good Deed,* 12.
51. Nancy Dubler, "Limiting Technology in the Process of Negotiating Death," *Yale Journal of Health Policy, Law, and Ethics* 1, no. 1 (January 9, 2013).
52. Palliative Care and End-of-Life Distribution of Information Regarding Availability, Massachusetts General Laws: Section 227, https://malegislature.gov/Laws/GeneralLaws/PartI/TitleXVI/Chapter111/Section227.

53. The Michigan Dignified Act 368 of 1978 of the Public Health Code, Section 333.5652, http://www.legislature.mi.gov/(S(rez2tlaa0fbv0oqn qx1lg5ad))/documents/mcl/pdf/mcl-368-1978-5-56A.pdf.

54. The End of Life Option Act, Assembly Bill No. 15, https://leginfo.legislature.ca.gov/faces/billNavClient.xhtml?bill_id=201520162AB15.

55. Palliative Care Information Act, Laws of New York, 2010 Chapter 331, www.health.ny.gov.

56. Atul Gawande, *Being Mortal: Illness, Medicine and What Matters in the End* (London: Profile Books in association with Wellcome Collection, 2014), 6.

57. The Conversation Project, https://theconversationproject.org.

58. Ira Byock, *The Best Care Possible: A Physician's Quest to Transform Care through the End of Life* (New York: Avery, 2012).

59. Rebecca Dresser, ed., *Malignant: Medical Ethicists Confront Cancer* (Oxford: Oxford University Press, 2012), 215.

60. Amy Paturel, "Let's Talk about Death," Association of American Medical Colleges, January 14, 2019, https://www.aamc.org/news-insights/let-s-talk-about-death.

61. "Most Patients Have Too Little Time in Hospice," April 17, 2019, https://www.1800hospice.com/blog/most-patients-have-too-little-time-in-hospice/#:~:text=The%20NHPCO%20releases%20periodic%20reports,get%20less%20than%20180%20days.

62. Medicare Care Choice Model, June 25, 2020, https://innovation.cms.gov/innovation-models/medicare-care-choices.

63. Danielle Scheurer, "Do Hospitalists Improve Patient Outcomes?" *The Hospitalist*, April 17, 2018.

64. Paturel, "Let's Talk about Death."

65. Paturel, "Let's Talk about Death."

66. Joe Klein, "The Long Goodbye," *Time Magazine*, July 11, 2012, 20.

67. Francis Peabody, "The Care of the Patient," *Journal of the American Medical Association*, March 19, 1927.

68. Robert Pearl, "Healthcare's Dangerous Fee-for-Service Addiction," *Forbes Magazine*, September 25, 2017.

69. "Racism as a Public Health Crisis," *Cornell Health*, https://health.cornell.edu/initiatives/skorton-center/racism-public-health-crisis.

70. Austin Frakt, "Bad Medicine: The Harm That Comes from Racism," *New York Times*, January 13, 2020.

71. Ken Alltucker, "US Doctor Shortage Worsens as Efforts to Recruit Black and Latino Students Stall," *USA Today,* June 26, 2020.

72. Right to Try Act, Food and Drug Administration, https://www.fda.gov /patients/learn-about-expanded-access-and-other-treatment-options /right-try.

73. Arthur Caplan, Kelly McBride Folkers, and Andrew McFayden, "A Bizarre Claim of Right to Try," *The Health Care Blog,* January 18, 2019, https://thehealthcareblog.com/blog/2019/01/18/a-bizarre-claim-of -right-to-try.

74. Jennifer Miller, "Boom Time for Death Planning," *New York Times,* July 16, 2020.

75. Miller, "Boom Time for Death Planning."

76. Trusted Decision Maker, https://www.instituteforhumancaring.org /Advance-Care-Planning.aspx.

77. Cavallo, "Using Video Support Tools."

78. "Six Fun Games to Help You Talk about End-of-Life Care," The Conversation Project, November 11, 2019, https://theconversationproject.org /tcp-blog/death-is-not-a-game-well-sometimes-it-is.

79. https://deathcafe.com.

80. http://www.orderofthegooddeath.com.

81. Alfred Killilea, *The Politics of Being Mortal* (Lexington: University Press of Kentucky, 2014), 8.

2. ON SNOWFLAKES, CHILLY CLIMATES, AND SHOUTING TO BE HEARD

1. Michael L. Shenkman, "URI Paper Faces Charges of Racism," *The Crimson,* December 9, 1998.

2. Shenkman, "URI Paper Faces Charges of Racism."

3. Shenkman, "URI Paper Faces Charges of Racism."

4. Shenkman, "URI Paper Faces Charges of Racism."

5. Janet Kerlin, "Cartoon Causes Racial Tension at URI," December 11, 1998, https://apnews.com/article/e5ce5dd5972ecb7e5e42eb2785cf8457.

6. Martin E. Comas, "UCF Protestors Demand Professor Be Fired for Racist Tweets," *Orlando Sentinel,* June 14, 2020.

7. Comas, "UCF Protestors Demand Professor Be Fired for Racist Tweets."

8. Comas, "UCF Protestors Demand Professor Be Fired for Racist Tweets."

9. Elizabeth Redden, "Offensive but Forgivable Joke or Fireable Offense?" *Inside Higher Ed,* August 26, 2020.

10. Redden, "Offensive but Forgivable Joke or Fireable Offense?"

11. Redden, "Offensive but Forgivable Joke or Fireable Offense?"

12. Greg Piper, "Mizzou Professor Removed from Teaching for Joking with Wuhan Student: 'Let Me Get My Mask On,'" *College Fix,* August 25, 2020.

13. Denise Magner, "Wisconsin Student Complains about Professor's Use of the Word 'Niggardly,'" *Chronicle of Higher Education.* February 12, 1999.

14. Tom Bartlett, "How One Word Led to an Uproar," *Chronicle of Higher Education,* September 17, 2020.

15. Bartlett, "How One Word Led to an Uproar."

16. Bartlett, "How One Word Led to an Uproar."

17. Colleen Flaherty, "Failure to Communicate," *Inside Higher Ed,* September 8, 2020.

18. Association of American Colleges and Universities and American Association of University Professors, "1940 Statement of Principles on Academic Freedom and Tenure," http://www.aaup.org.

19. Association of American Colleges and Universities and American Association of University Professors, "1940 Statement of Principles on Academic Freedom and Tenure."

20. Pen America, *Chasm in the Classroom,* April 2019, https://pen.org/chasm-in-the-classroom-campus-free-speech-in-a-divided-america.

21. Christie Aschwanden, "How 'Superspreader' Events Drive Most COVID-19 Spread," *Scientific American,* June 23, 2020.

22. Lilah Burke, "Professor on Leave after Statement on Trump Supporters," *Inside Higher Ed,* September 21, 2020.

23. Dominick Mastrangelo, "Professor Suspended for Telling Students She Hopes Trump Supporters Catch Coronavirus and Die," *The Hill,* September 18, 2020.

24. Mastrangelo, "Professor Suspended for Telling Students She Hopes Trump Supporters Catch Coronavirus and Die."

25. Pen America, *Chasm.*

26. Pen America, *Chasm.*

27. Liz Clarke and Des Bieler, "NASCAR Bans Display of Confederate Flag at All Event and Properties," *Washington Post,* June 10, 2020.

28. Rachel Treisman, "The NFL Will Play 'Lift Every Voice and Sing' before Each Season Opener Game," NPR, July 2, 2020, audio.

29. David Hessekiel, "Companies Taking a Public Stand in the Wake of George Floyd's Death," *Forbes,* June 4, 2020.

30. Hessekiel, "Companies Taking a Public Stand in the Wake of George Floyd's Death."

31. Hessekiel, "Companies Taking a Public Stand in the Wake of George Floyd's Death."

32. Tiffany Hsu, "Aunt Jemima Brand to Change Name and Image over 'Racial Stereotype,'" *New York Times,* June 17, 2020.

33. Erik Brady, "Daniel Snyder Says Redskins Will Never Change Name," *USA Today,* May 9, 2013.

34. Marc Stein, "Led by N.B.A., Boycotts Disrupt Pro Sports in Wake of Blake Shooting," *New York Times,* August 29, 2020.

35. Michael Wines and Aishvarya Kavi, "March on Washington 2020: Protesters Hope to Rekindle Spirit of 1963," *New York Times,* August 28, 2020.

36. Jason England and Richard Purcell, "Higher Ed's Toothless Response to the Killing of George Floyd," *Chronicle of Higher Education,* June 8, 2020.

37. Francie Diep, "'I Was Fed Up': How #BlackintheIvory Got Started, and What Its Founders Want to See Next," *Chronicle of Higher Education,* June 9, 2020.

38. Association of American Colleges and Universities and ABC Insights, "Responding to the Ongoing COVID-19 Crisis and to Calls for Racial Justice: A Survey of College and University Presidents," August 3, 2020, https://www.aacu.org/sites/default/files/files/research/AACU_ABC _PTSurvey_Report_Findings_updated.pdf.

39. Association of American Colleges and Universities and ABC Insights, "Responding to the Ongoing COVID-19 Crisis and to Calls for Racial Justice."

40. Association of American Colleges and Universities, *What Liberal Education Looks Like: What It Is, Who It's For, and Where It Happens,* https:// www.aacu.org/what-liberal-education-looks-0.

41. Lynn Pasquerella, "Rewriting the Dominant Narrative: How Liberal Education Can Advance Racial Healing and Transformation," *Liberal Education* 102 (Fall 2016): 16.

42. Scott Jaschik, "The Chicago Letter and Its Aftermath," *Inside Higher Ed*, August 29, 2016.

43. George Will, "On American Campuses, Freedom from Speech," *Washington Post*, November 13, 2015.

44. Jaschik, "The Chicago Letter."

45. Jaschik, "The Chicago Letter."

46. Chris Quintana, "Colleges Are Creating 'a Generation of Sanctimonious, Sensitive, Supercilious Snowflakes,' Sessions Says," *Chronicle of Higher Education*, July 24, 2018.

47. Scott Jaschik, "DeVos vs. the Faculty," *Inside Higher Ed*, February 24, 2017.

48. Pen America, *Chasm*.

49. Joan Scott, "How the Right Weaponized Free Speech," *Chronicle of Higher Education*, January 7, 2018.

50. The Goldwater Institute, "Restoring Free Speech on Campus," 2017, https://www.goldwaterinstitute.org.

51. Laura Meckler and Valerie Strauss, "Government Threatens Funding for Middle East Studies Program It Sees as Too Favorable to Islam," *Washington Post*, September 19, 2019.

52. Remarks by President Trump at Signing of Executive Order, "Improving Free Inquiry, Transparency, and Accountability at Colleges and Universities," March 21, 2019, http://www.whitehouse.gov.

53. Emma Goldberg, "Hong Kong Protests Spread to U.S. Colleges, and a Rift Grows," *New York Times*, October 26, 201.

54. Kathleen McWilliams, "In Lawsuit against Wesleyan, Professor Accuses School of Failing to Protect Him from 'Slanderous and Vicious Personal Attacks' Labeling Him A Sex Offender," *Hartford Courant*, August 29, 2019.

55. Nick Hazelrigg, "Expensive Aftermath of Protests," *Inside Higher Ed*, June 10, 2019.

56. Colleen Flaherty, "Don't 'Go There.'" *Inside Higher Ed*, February 24, 2016.

57. Ruthie Blum, "'Zionists Out of CUNY' 'Long Live the Intifada' Chanted at CUNY Student Protest at Hunter," *The Algemeiner*, https://www.algemeiner.com/2015/11/13/zionists-out-of-cuny-long-live-the-intifada-chanted-at-cuny-student-protest-at-hunter-administration-looks-other-way.

58. Patricia McGuire, "Whose Freedom of Speech?" *Inside Higher Ed*, March 27, 2019.

59. "Seven Dirty Words, According to the Trump Administration," editorial, *Washington Post,* December 18, 2017.

60. Paul Fain, "Trump Threatens Tax Exemption of Colleges," *Inside Higher Ed,* July 13, 2020.

61. Jack Blum, "Executive Order Prohibits Federal Contractors and Grantees from Using Many Forms of Diversity and Implicit Bias Training," *National Law Review* 10, no. 267 (September 23, 2020).

62. Blum, "Executive Order Prohibits Federal Contractors."

63. Daniel Bergner, "'White Fragility' Is Everywhere: But Does Antiracism Training Work?" *Washington Post,* July 17, 2020.

64. Kery Murakami, "College Leaders Back Princeton in Civil Rights Probe," *Inside Higher Ed,* September 25, 2020.

65. Evan Gerstmann, "Trump Says He Will Punish Schools That Teach the *New York Times*' '1619' Project by Withholding Federal Funds," *Forbes Magazine,* September 2020.

66. Blum, "Executive Order Prohibits Federal Contractors."

67. Susan Svrluga, "Scores of College Presidents Urge Education Department to Stop Its Investigation of Princeton," *Washington Post,* September 25, 2020.

68. Adam Liptak, "How Conservatives Weaponized the First Amendment," *New York Times,* June 30, 2018.

69. Ulrich Baer, *What Snowflakes Get Right: Free Speech, Truth, and Equality on Campus* (Oxford: Oxford University Press, 2019), 6.

70. Baer, *What Snowflakes Get Right,* 68.

71. Pen America, *Chasm.*

72. Pen America, *Chasm.*

73. Pen America, *Chasm.*

74. Pen America, *Chasm.*

75. Pen America, *Chasm.*

76. American Psychological Association, "'We Are Living in a Racism Pandemic, Says APA President," May 29, 2020, https://www.apa.org/news/press/releases/2020/05/racism-pandemic.

77. Pen America, *Chasm.*

78. Lynn Pasquerella, "Free Expression, Liberal Education, and Inclusive Excellence," https://www.aacu.org/about/statements/2017/free-expression.

79. Aaron Randle, "Officials Call 'Redmen' a Racist Mascot: Then Voters Weighed In," *New York Times,* July 11, 2020.

80. "Killingly, Don't Revive the Racist Mascot," opinion editorial, *Hartford Courant*, December 10, 2019.
81. "Killingly, Don't Revive the Racist Mascot."
82. "Killingly, Don't Revive the Racist Mascot."
83. "Killingly, Don't Revive the Racist Mascot."
84. Linda Alcoff, "The Problem of Speaking for Others," *Cultural Critique*, no. 20 (Winter 1991–92): 5–32.
85. Alcoff, "The Problem of Speaking for Others."
86. Alcoff, "The Problem of Speaking for Others."
87. E. Patrick Johnson, *Appropriating Blackness: Performance and the Politics of Authenticity* (Durham, NC: Duke University Press, 2003).
88. Pasquerella, "Free Expression, Liberal Education and Inclusive Excellence."
89. Pasquerella, "Free Expression, Liberal Education and Inclusive Excellence."
90. Pasquerella, "Free Expression, Liberal Education and Inclusive Excellence."
91. Baer, *What Snowflakes Get Right*.
92. Mark Kingwell, "Campus Discord: Shout If You Must. But First Have Something to Say . . . ," *Globe and Mail*, November 21, 2015.
93. John Churchill, "What's a Core For? Varieties of Curricular Experience," September 26, 2014, https://www.coretexts.org.
94. Martha Nussbaum, *Not for Profit: Why Democracy Needs the Humanities* (Princeton. NJ: Princeton University Press, 2010), 95–120.

3. PREPARING STUDENTS FOR WORK, CITIZENSHIP, AND LIFE IN THE TWENTY-FIRST-CENTURY

1. "COVID-19 Stopout Student Survey: Key Insights," ReUp Education, May 2020, https://reupeducation.com/covid-19-stopout-student-survey-key-insights.
2. Scott Jaschik, "A Tough Year for Community Colleges," *Inside Higher Ed*, August 17, 2020.
3. "Higher Ed and COVID-19 National Student Survey Part III—The Fragility of Trust," SimpsonScarborough, August 2020, https://info.simpsonscarborough.com/hubfs/SimpsonScarborough%20National%20Student%20Survey,%20Pt.%20III.pdf.

4. Pell Institute 2020 Indicators of Higher Education in the US, http://pellinstitute.org/indicators/reports_2020.shtml.

5. Association of American Colleges and Universities, *What Liberal Education Looks Like,* Association of American Colleges and Universities, April 2020, https://www.aacu.org/what-liberal-education-looks-0.

6. Jeffrey M. Jones, "Confidence in Higher Education Down since 2015," October 9, 2018, https://news.gallup.com/opinion/gallup/242441 /confidence-higher-education-down-2015.aspx.

7. Kim Parker, "The Growing Partisan Divide in Views of Higher Education," Pew Research Center Social and Demographic Trends, August 19, 2019, https://www.pewresearch.org/social-trends/2019/08/19/the -growing-partisan-divide-in-views-of-higher-education-2.

8. Anna Brown, "Most Americans Say Higher Ed Is Heading in Wrong Direction, But Partisans Disagree on Why," July 26, 2018, https://www .pewresearch.org/fact-tank/2018/07/26/most-americans-say-higher-ed -is-heading-in-wrong-direction-but-partisans-disagree-on-why.

9. Brandon Busteed, "Importance of College Drops Nearly 50% among Young Adults in Just Six Years," *Forbes,* December 15, 2019.

10. Jeremy Wallace, "Rick Scott No Fan of Anthropology," *Sarasota Herald Tribune,* October 10, 2011.

11. Valerie Strauss, "N.C. Governor Attacks Higher Ed, Proposes Funding Colleges by Graduates' Jobs," *Washington Post,* February 7, 2013.

12. Scott Jaschik, "Trump's Emerging Higher Ed Platform," *Inside Higher Ed,* May 13, 2016.

13. Jennifer Epstein and Carrie Budoff Brown, "Obama: Review Training Programs," *Politico,* January 30, 2014.

14. Donald Trump, "Nevada Caucus Victory Speech," February 23, 2016, http://www.qz.com.

15. Portions of this essay are reprinted from the foreword of *Achieving the Dream: A How-to Guide for Adult Women Seeking a College Degree,* by Carol Leary (Amherst, MA: White River, 2016).

16. Benjamin Barber, "The Civic Mission of the University," *Kettering Review* (Fall 1989).

17. Excerpted from Lynn Pasquerella, "Trump, Loans and the Liberal Arts," *Inside Higher Ed,* July 29, 2016.

18. Pasquerella, foreword to *Achieving the Dream,* by Carol Leary.

19. David Sonious, *Divided We Fall* (New York: Page, 2017).

20. Sherry Linkon, "Working Class Voters," *The Academic Minute*, NPR, November 7, 2016, audio.
21. Linkon, "Working Class Voters."
22. Melissa Tokarczyk, "Hidden Anxieties of the White Working Class," *Working Class Perspectives*, December 19, 2016.
23. Jennifer Morton, *Moving up without Losing Your Way: The Ethical Costs of Upward Mobility* (Princeton, NJ: Princeton University Press, 2019).
24. Chuck Wibby, "From the Editorial Advisory Board: 'Liberal' Not Always Political," *Colorado Daily Camera*, June 29, 2018.
25. Amy Olberding, "How Useful Is Imposter Syndrome in Academia?" *Aeon*, March 2018.
26. Olberding, "How Useful Is Imposter Syndrome in Academia?"
27. Michael Sandel, "Disdain for the Less Educated is the Last Acceptable Prejudice," *New York Times*, September 2, 2020.
28. Sandel, "Disdain for the Less Educated is the Last Acceptable Prejudice."
29. Michael Sandel, *The Tyranny of Merit: What's Become of the Common Good?* (New York: Penguin, 2020).
30. Sandel, *The Tyranny of Merit.*
31. Association of American Colleges and Universities, "Fulfilling the American Dream: Liberal Education and the Future of Work," 2018, https://www.aacu.org/sites/default/files/files/LEAP/2018EmployerResearchReport.pdf.
32. Association of American Colleges and Universities, "Fulfilling the American Dream."
33. Association of American Colleges and Universities, "Fulfilling the American Dream."
34. National Academies of Sciences, Engineering, and Medicine, *The Integration of the Humanities and Arts with Sciences, Engineering and Medicine in Higher Education: Branches from the Same Tree* (Washington, DC: National Academies Press, 2018), 9.
35. National Academies of Sciences, Engineering, and Medicine, *The Integration of the Humanities and Arts with Sciences, Engineering and Medicine in Higher Education*, 9.
36. National Academies of Sciences, Engineering, and Medicine, *The Integration of the Humanities and Arts with Sciences, Engineering and Medicine in Higher Education*, 9.

37. National Academies of Sciences, Engineering, and Medicine, *The Integration of the Humanities and Arts with Sciences, Engineering and Medicine in Higher Education*, 54.

38. National Academies of Sciences, Engineering, and Medicine, *The Integration of the Humanities and Arts with Sciences, Engineering and Medicine in Higher Education*, 54.

39. Lynn Pasquerella, "Scientism, Human Consciousness and the STIRS Imperative," *Peer Review* 18, no. 4 (Fall 2016).

40. Pasquerella, "Scientism, Human Consciousness and the STIRS Imperative."

41. Lee Benson, Ira Harkay, John Puckett, Matthew Hartley, Rita A. Hodges, Francis E. Johnston, and Joann Weeks, *Knowledge for Social Change: Bacon, Dewey, and the Revolutionary Transformation of Research Universities in the Twenty-First Century* (Philadelphia: Temple University Press, 2017).

42. Jill Lepore, "Franklin, Reconsidered: An Essay by Jill Lepore," *Longreads*, September 2015.

43. Ronald Dworkin, *Is Democracy Possible Here? Principles for a New Political Debate* (Princeton, NJ: Princeton University Press, 2006), 6.

44. See Lynn Pasquerella, "In Pursuit of Quality and Deliberative Democracy," *Liberal Education* 104, no. 2 (Spring 2018).

45. José Bowen, "A New Year's Resolution for 'The Age of Certainty,'" *The Hill*, December 31, 2020.

46. Association of American Colleges and Universities, *What Liberal Education Looks Like*.

47. Anthony P. Carnevale, Nicole Smith, Lenka Dražanova, Artim Gulish, and Kathryn Peltier Campbell, *The Role of Education in Taming Authoritarian Attitudes*, Georgetown University Center on Education and the Workforce, https://cew.georgetown.edu/cew-reports/authoritarianism.

48. Lynn Pasquerella, "Liberal Education and Threats to Democracy," *Liberal Education* (Fall/Winter 2020).

49. Pasquerella, "Liberal Education and Threats to Democracy."

50. Carnevale, Smith, Dražanova, Gulish, and Campbell, *The Role of Education*.

51. Carnevale, Smith, Dražanova, Gulish, and Campbell, *The Role of Education*.

52. Carnevale, Smith, Dražanova, Gulish, and Campbell, *The Role of Education*.

53. Michael Roth, "Shaping Spaces Safe Enough for Pragmatic Liberal Education: Pressures and Possibilities," Association of American Colleges and Universities 2020 Annual Meeting, Washington, DC, January 25, 2020.

54. Cathy N. Davidson, "Why We Need a New Higher Education: We Have a Responsibility to the Next Generation of Students," *Liberal Education* 105, no. 2 (Spring 2019).

55. Davidson, "Why We Need a New Higher Education."

56. Association of American Colleges and Universities, *What Liberal Education Looks Like.*

57. Anemona Hartocollis, "University of California Is Sued over Use of SAT and ACT in Admissions," *New York Times,* December 10, 2019.

58. Maria Popova, "How to Listen between the Lines: Anna Deavere Smith on the Art of Listening in a Culture of Speaking," *Brain Pickings*, January 29, 2015.

59. Mark Twain, *Notebook* (New York: Cooper Square, 1908).

60. Mark Kingwell, "A Populist Wake-Up Call for Universities," *Academic Matters,* Spring 2017.

BIBLIOGRAPHY

Alcoff, Linda. "The Problem of Speaking for Others." *Cultural Critique,* no. 20 (Winter 1991–92): 5–32.

Alltucker, Ken. "US Doctor Shortage Worsens as Efforts to Recruit Black and Latino Students Stall." *USA Today,* June 26, 2020.

Alsan, Marcella, and Marianne Wanamaker. "Tuskegee and the Health of Black Men." June 2016. National Bureau of Economic Research. https://www.nber.org/papers/w22323.

American Medical Association. *American Medical Association Code of Ethics.* Chicago: American Medical Association Press, 1847.

——. American Medical Association Code of Ethics. June 2016. www.ama-assn.org/delivering-care/ethics/ama-code-medical-ethics-guidance-pandemic.

American Psychological Association. "'We Are Living in a Racism Pandemic,' Says APA President." May 29, 2020. https://www.apa.org/news/press/releases/2020/05/racism-pandemic.

Annas, George. "How We Lie." *The Hastings Center Report.* November/December 1995. https://www.onlinelibrary.wiley.com.

Arato v. Avedon. Court of Appeal, Second District, Division 3, California, 1992. https://caselaw.findlaw.com/ca-court-of-appeal/1759004.html.

Aschwanden, Christie. "How 'Superspreader' Events Drive Most COVID-19 Spread." *Scientific American,* June 23, 2020.

Association of American Colleges and Universities. *What Liberal Education Looks Like: What It Is, Who It's For, and Where It Happens.* Association of American Colleges and Universities, April 2020. https://www.aacu.org/what-liberal-education-looks-0.

Association of American Colleges and Universities and ABC Insights.
"Responding to the Ongoing COVID-19 Crisis and to Calls for Racial
Justice A Survey of College and University Presidents." August 3, 2020.
https://www.aacu.org/sites/default/files/files/research/AACU_ABC
_PTSurvey_Report_Findings__updated.pdf.

Association of American Colleges and Universities and American Association of University Professors. "1940 Statement of Principles on Academic
Freedom and Tenure." https://www.aaup.org/report/1940-statement
-principles-academic-freedom-and-tenure.

Association of American Colleges and Universities and Hart Research
Associates. "Fulfilling the American Dream: Liberal Education and the
Future of Work." 2018. https://www.aacu.org/sites/default/files/files
/LEAP/2018EmployerResearchReport.pdf.

Baer, Ulrich. *What Snowflakes Get Right: Free Speech, Truth, and Equality on
Campus.* Oxford: Oxford University Press, 2019.

Barber, Benjamin. "The Civic Mission of the University." *Kettering Review*
(Fall 1989).

Bartlett, Tom. "How One Word Led to an Uproar." *Chronicle of Higher Education,* September 17, 2020.

Benson, Lee, Ira Harkay, John Puckett, Matthew Hartley, Rita A. Hodges,
Francis E. Johnston, and Joann Weeks. *Knowledge for Social Change:
Bacon, Dewey, and the Revolutionary Transformation of Research Uni-
versities in the Twenty-First Century.* Philadelphia: Temple University
Press, 2017.

Bergner, Daniel. "'White Fragility' Is Everywhere: But Does Antiracism
Training Work?" *Washington Post,* July 17, 2020.

Blum, Jack. "Executive Order Prohibits Federal Contractors and Grantees from Using Many Forms of Diversity and Implicit Bias Training."
National Law Review 10, no. 267 (September 23, 2020).

Blum, Ruthie. "'Zionists Out of CUNY' 'Long Live the Intifada' Chanted
at CUNY Student Protest at Hunter." *The Algemeiner.* https://www
.algemeiner.com/2015/11/13/zionists-out-of-cuny-long-live-the-intifada
-chanted-at-cuny-student-protest-at-hunter-administration-looks-other
-way.

Bowen, José. "A New Year's Resolution for 'The Age of Certainty.'" *The Hill,*
December 31, 2020.

Brady, Erik. "Daniel Snyder Says Redskins Will Never Change Name." *USA
Today,* May 9, 2013.

Brice-Saddler, Michael. "Memorial Held Outside White House in Solemn Reminder of More Than 200,000 Americans Killed by COVID-19." *Washington Post,* October 4, 2020.

Brown, Anna. "Most Americans Say Higher Ed Is Heading in Wrong Direction, but Partisans Disagree on Why." Pew Research. July 26, 2018. https://www.pewresearch.org/fact-tank/2018/07/26/most-americans-say-higher-ed-is-heading-in-wrong-direction-but-partisans-disagree-on-why.

Burke, Lilah. "Professor on Leave after Statement on Trump Supporters." *Inside Higher Ed,* September 21, 2020.

Busteed, Brandon. "Importance of College Drops Nearly 50% among Young Adults in Just Six Years." *Forbes,* December 15, 2019.

Byok, Ira. *The Best Care Possible: A Physician's Quest to Transform Care through the End of Life.* New York: Avery, 2012.

Caplan, Arthur, Kelly McBride Folkers, and Andrew McFayden. "A Bizarre Claim of Right to Try." *Health Care Blog,* January 18, 2019.

Carnevale, Anthony P., Nicole Smith, Lenka Dražanova, Artim Gulish, and Kathryn Peltier Campbell. *The Role of Education in Taming Authoritarian Attitudes.* Georgetown University Center on Education and the Workforce. https://cew.georgetown.edu/cew-reports/authoritarianism.

Cavallo, Jo. "Using Video Support Tools to Facilitate End-of-Life Discussions with Patients: A Conversation with Angelo E. Volandes, MD, MPH." *ASCO Post,* May 10, 2018.

Centers for Disease Control. "COVID-19 in Racial and Ethnic Minority Groups." June 25, 2020. https://www.cdc.gov/coronavirus/2019-ncov/community/health-equity/racial-ethnic-disparities/index.html.

Chomilo, Nathan, Nia Heard-Garris, Malini DeSilva, and Uché Blackstock. "The Harm of a Colorblind Allocation of Scarce Resources." *Health Affairs,* April 30, 2020.

Churchill, John. "What's a Core For? Varieties of Curricular Experience." September 14, 2014. https://www.coretexts.org.

Churchill, Larry R. *Ethics for Everyone: A Skills-Based Approach.* Oxford: Oxford University Press, 2019.

Clarke, Liz, and Des Bieler. "NASCAR Bans Display of Confederate Flag at All Event and Properties." *Washington Post,* June 10, 2020.

Cohen, Lewis M. *No Good Deed: A Story of Medicine, Murder Accusations, and the Debate over How We Die.* New York: HarperCollins, 2010.

Comas, Martin E. "UCF Protestors Demand Professor Be Fired for Racist Tweets." *Orlando Sentinel,* June 14, 2020.

Connors, Alfred F., Neal V. Dawson, and Norman A. Desbiens, et al. "A Controlled Trial to Improve Care for Seriously Ill Hospitalized Patients: The Study to Understand Prognoses and Preferences for Outcomes and Risks of Treatments (SUPPORT)." *Journal of the American Medical Association* 274, no. 20 (1995): 1591–98.

Corley, M. C. "Nurse Moral Distress: A Proposed Theory and Research Agenda." *Nursing Ethics* 9, no. 6 (November 2002): 636–50.

The Conversation Project. https://theconversationproject.org.

Davidson, Cathy N. "Why We Need a New Higher Education: We Have a Responsibility to the Next Generation of Students." *Liberal Education* 105, no. 2 (Spring 2019).

De Botton, Alain. "Camus on the Coronavirus." *New York Times,* March 19, 2020.

Dean, Wendy, and Simon Talbot. "Moral Injury and Burnout in Medicine: A Year of Lessons Learned." *STAT,* July 26, 2019.

Diep, Francie. "'I Was Fed Up': How #BlackintheIvory Got Started, and What Its Founders Want to See Next." *Chronicle of Higher Education,* June 9, 2020.

Dresser, Rebecca, ed. *Malignant: Medical Ethicists Confront Cancer.* Oxford: Oxford University Press, 2012.

Dubler, Nancy. "Limiting Technology in the Process of Negotiating Death." *Yale Journal of Health Policy, Law, and Ethics* 1, no. 1 (January 9, 2013).

Dworkin, Ronald. *Is Democracy Possible Here? Principles for a New Political Debate.* Princeton, NJ: Princeton University Press, 2006.

End of Life Option Act. Assembly Bill No. 15. https://leginfo.legislature.ca .gov/faces/billNavClient.xhtml?bill_id=201520162AB15.

England, Jason, and Richard Purcell. "Higher Ed's Toothless Response to the Killing of George Floyd." *Chronicle of Higher Education,* June 8, 2020.

Epstein, Jennifer, and Carrie Budoff Brown. "Obama: Review Training Programs." *Politico,* January 30, 2014.

Fain, Paul. "Trump Threatens Tax Exemption of Colleges." *Inside Higher Ed,* July 13, 2020.

Farmer, Blake. "When Doctors Struggle with Suicide, Their Profession Often Fails Them." *Morning Edition,* NPR, July 31, 2018. Audio.

Flaherty, Colleen. "Don't 'Go There.'" *Inside Higher Ed,* February 24, 2016.

———. "Failure to Communicate." *Inside Higher Ed,* September 8, 2020.

Food and Drug Administration. Right to Try Act. https://www.fda.gov
/patients/learn-about-expanded-access-and-other-treatment-options
/right-try.

Frakt, Austin. "Bad Medicine: The Harm That Comes from Racism." *New York Times,* January 13, 2020.

Gawande, Atul. *Being Mortal: Illness, Medicine and What Matters in the End.* London: Profile Books in association with Wellcome Collection, 2014.

Gerstmann, Evan. "Trump Says He Will Punish Schools That Teach *The New York Times'* '1619' Project by Withholding Federal Funds." *Forbes Magazine,* September 2020.

Goldberg, Emma. "Hong Kong Protests Spread to U.S. Colleges, and a Rift Grows." *New York Times,* October 26, 2019.

Goldwater Institute. "Restoring Free Speech on Campus." 2017. https://www.goldwaterinstitute.org.

Groopman, Jerome. *The Anatomy of Hope: How People Prevail in the Face of Illness.* New York: Random House, 2005.

Harper, Jake. "As COVID-19 Spreads, It's Time to Discuss End of Life Plan." *Side Effects: Public Health Personal Stories.* WFYI Live Radio. April 6, 2020. Audio. https://www.sideeffectspublicmedia.org/access-to-healthcare/2020-04-03/as-covid-19-spreads-its-time-to-discuss-end-of-life-plan.

Hartocollis, Anemona. "University of California Is Sued over Use of SAT and ACT in Admissions." *New York Times,* December 10, 2019.

Hazelrigg, Nick. "Expensive Aftermath of Protests." *Inside Higher Ed,* June 10, 2019.

Hessekiel, David. "Companies Taking a Public Stand in the Wake of George Floyd's Death." *Forbes,* June 4, 2020.

Holan, Angie Drobnic. "PolitiFact's Lie of the Year: 'Death Panels.'" *PolitiFact,* December 18, 2009.

Hsu, Tiffany. "Aunt Jemima Brand to Change Name and Image over 'Racial Stereotype.'" *New York Times,* June 17, 2020.

Jaschik, Scott. "The Chicago Letter and Its Aftermath." *Inside Higher Ed,* August 29, 2016.

———. "DeVos vs. the Faculty." *Inside Higher Ed,* February 24, 2017.

———. "A Tough Year for Community Colleges." *Inside Higher Ed,* August 17, 2020.

———. "Trump's Emerging Higher Ed Platform." *Inside Higher Ed,* May 13, 2016.

Johnson, E. Patrick. *Appropriating Blackness: Performance and the Politics of Authenticity.* Durham, NC: Duke University Press, 2003.

Jones, Jeffrey M. "Confidence in Higher Education down since 2015." October 9, 2018. https://news.gallup.com/opinion/gallup/242441/confidence-higher-education-down-2015.aspx.

Kerlin, Janet. "Cartoon Causes Racial Tension at URI." December 11, 1998. https://apnews.com/article/e5ce5dd5972ecb7e5e42eb2785cf8457.

Killilea, Alfred. *The Politics of Being Mortal.* Lexington: University Press of Kentucky, 2014.

"Killingly, Don't Revive the Racist Mascot." Opinion editorial. *Hartford Courant,* December 10, 2019. http://www.Courant.com/opinion/editorials/hc-ed-killingly-highschool-redmen-redhawks-mascot-121020191210.

Kingwell, Mark. "Campus Discord: Shout if You Must. But First Have Something to Say. . . ." *Globe and Mail,* November 21, 2015.

———. "A Populist Wake-Up Call for Universities." *Academic Matters,* Spring 2017.

Klein, Joe. "The Long Goodbye." *Time Magazine,* July 11, 2012, 20.

Lai, Jianbo, Simeng Ma, Ying Wang, et al. "Factors Associated with Mental Health Outcomes among Health Care Workers Exposed to Coronavirus Disease 2019." *Journal of the American Medical Association,* March 23, 2020.

Lepore, Jill. "Franklin, Reconsidered: An Essay by Jill Lepore." *Longreads,* September 2015.

Linkon, Sherry. "Working Class Voters." *The Academic Minute.* NPR. November 7, 2016. Audio.

Liptak, Adam. "How Conservatives Weaponized the First Amendment." *New York Times,* June 30, 2018.

Machado, Amanda. "Why Many Latinos Dread Going to the Doctor." *The Atlantic,* May 7, 2014.

Magner, Denise. "Wisconsin Student Complains about Professor's Use of the Word 'Niggardly.'" *Chronicle of Higher Education,* February 12, 1999.

Mastrangelo, Dominick. "Professor Suspended for Telling Students She Hopes Trump Supporters Catch Coronavirus and Die." *The Hill,* September 18, 2020.

McCabe, Mary S., and Courtney Storm. "When Doctors and Patients Disagree about Medical Futility." *Journal of Oncological Practice* 4, no. 4 (July 4, 2008).

McGuire, Patricia. "Whose Freedom of Speech?" *Inside Higher Ed,* March 27, 2019.

McWilliams, Kathleen. "In Lawsuit against Wesleyan, Professor Accuses School of Failing to Protect Him from 'Slanderous and Vicious Personal Attacks' Labeling Him a Sex Offender." *Hartford Courant,* August 29, 2019.

Meckler, Laura, and Valerie Strauss. "Government Threatens Funding for Middle East Studies Program It Sees as Too Favorable to Islam." *Washington Post,* September 19, 2019.

Medicare Care Choice Model. June 25, 2020. https://innovation.cms.gov /innovation-models/medicare-care-choices.

The Michigan Dignified Act 368 of 1978 of the Public Health Code, Section 333.5652. http://www.legislature.mi.gov/(S(rez2tlaa0fbv0oqnqx1lg5ad)) /documents/mcl/pdf/mcl-368-1978-5-56A.pdf.

Miller, Jennifer. "Boom Time for Death Planning." *New York Times,* July 16, 2020.

The Moral Machine Game. https://www.moralmachine.net.

Morton, Jennifer. *Moving up without Losing Your Way: The Ethical Costs of Upward Mobility.* Princeton, NJ: Princeton University Press, 2019.

"Most Patients Have Too Little Time in Hospice." April 17, 2019. https:// www.1800hospice.com/blog/most-patients-have-too-little-time-in -hospice/#:~:text=The%20NHPCO%20releases%20periodic%20reports ,get%20less%20than%20180%20days.

Murakami, Kery. "College Leaders Back Princeton in Civil Rights Probe." *Inside Higher Ed,* September 25, 2020.

National Academies of Sciences, Engineering, and Medicine. *The Integration of the Humanities and Arts with Sciences, Engineering, and Medicine in Higher Education: Branches from the Same Tree.* Washington, DC: National Academies Press, 2018.

Nuland, Sherwin. *How We Die: Reflections on Life's Final Chapter.* New York: Penguin, 1994.

Nussbaum, Martha. *Not for Profit: Why Democracy Needs the Humanities.* Princeton, NJ: Princeton University Press, 2010.

Olberding, Amy. "How Useful Is Imposter Syndrome in Academia?" *Aeon* (March 2018).

The Order of the Good Death. http://www.orderofthegooddeath.com.

Palliative Care and End-of-Life Distribution of Information Regarding Availability. Massachusetts General Laws: Section 227. https://

malegislature.gov/Laws/GeneralLaws/PartI/TitleXVI/Chapter111 /Section227.

Palliative Care Information Act. Laws of New York, 2010 Chapter 331. www .health.ny.gov.

Parker, Kim. "The Growing Partisan Divide in Views of Higher Education." Pew Research Center Social and Demographic Trends. August 19, 2019. https://www.pewresearch.org/social-trends/2019/08/19/the-growing -partisan-divide-in-views-of-higher-education-2.

Pasquerella, Lynn. Foreword to *Achieving the Dream: A How-to Guide for Adult Women Seeking a College Degree,* by Carol Leary. Amherst, MA: White River, 2016.

———. "Free Expression, Liberal Education, and Inclusive Excellence." https://www.aacu.org/about/statements/2017/free-expression.

———. "In Pursuit of Quality and Deliberative Democracy." *Liberal Education* (Spring 2018).

———. "Liberal Education and Threats to Democracy." *Liberal Education* (Fall/Winter 2020).

———. "Rewriting the Dominant Narrative: How Liberal Education Can Advance Racial Healing and Transformation." *Liberal Education.* (Fall 2016).

———. "Scientism, Human Consciousness and the STIRS Imperative," *Peer Review* (Fall 2016).

———. "Trump, Loans and the Liberal Arts." *Inside Higher Ed,* July 29, 2016.

Paturel, Amy. "Let's Talk about Death." Association of American Medical Colleges. January 14, 2019. https://www.aamc.org/news-insights/let-s -talk-about-death.

Peabody, Francis. "The Care of the Patient." *Journal of the American Medical Association,* March 19, 1927.

Pearl, Robert. "Healthcare's Dangerous Fee-for-Service Addiction." *Forbes Magazine,* September 25, 2017.

Pell Institute 2020 Indicators of Higher Education in the US. http://pellinstitute.org/indicators/reports_2020.shtml.

Pen America. *Chasm in the Classroom.* April 2019. https://pen.org/chasm-in -the-classroom-campus-free-speech-in-a-divided-america.

Piper, Greg. "Mizzou Professor Removed from Teaching for Joking with Wuhan Student: 'Let Me Get My Mask On." *College Fix,* August 25, 2020.

Popova, Maria. "How to Listen between the Lines: Anna Deavere Smith on the Art of Listening in a Culture of Speaking." *Brain Pickings*, January 29, 2015.

Portanova, Jaclyn, Jennifer Allshire, Catherine Perez, Anna Rahman, and Susan Enguidanos. "Ethnic Difference in Advance Care Directive Completion and Care Preferences: What Has Changed in a Decade?" *Journal of the American Geriatric Society* 65, no. 6 (March 9, 2017).

Quintana, Chris. "Colleges Are Creating 'a Generation of Sanctimonious, Sensitive, Supercilious Snowflakes,' Sessions Says." *Chronicle of Higher Education*, July 24, 2018.

"Racism as a Public Health Crisis." Cornell Health. https://health.cornell .edu/initiatives/skorton-center/racism-public-health-crisis.

Randle, Aaron. "Officials Call 'Redmen' a Racist Mascot: Then Voters Weighed In." *New York Times*, July 11, 2020.

Redden, Elizabeth. "Offensive but Forgivable Joke or Fireable Offense?" *Inside Higher Ed*, August 26, 2020.

ReUp Education. "COVID-19 Stopout Student Survey: Key Insights." May 2020. https://reupeducation.com/covid-19-stopout-student-survey-key -insights.

Robert Wood Johnson Foundation. "Before I Die." https://www.thirteen .org/bid/p-johnson.html.

Roth, Michael. "Shaping Spaces Safe Enough for Pragmatic Liberal Education: Pressures and Possibilities." Association of American Colleges and Universities 2020 Annual Meeting, Washington, DC. January 25, 2020.

Sandel, Michael. "Disdain for the Less Educated is the Last Acceptable Prejudice." *New York Times*, September 2, 2020.

———. *The Tyranny of Merit: What's Become of the Common Good?* New York: Penguin, 2020.

Scheurer, Danielle. "Do Hospitalists Improve Patient Outcomes?" *The Hospitalist*, April 17, 2018. https://blog.hospitalmedicine.org/do-hospitalists -improve-inpatient-outcomes.

Schulte, Grant. "Michigan Governor Says Trump's Words Inspire Extremists." *Washington Post*, October 8, 2020.

Scott, Joan. "How the Right Weaponized Free Speech." *Chronicle of Higher Education*, January 7, 2018.

"Seven Dirty Words, According to the Trump Administration." Editorial. *Washington Post*, December 18, 2017.

Shenkman, Michael L. "URI Paper Faces Charges of Racism." *The Crimson,* December 9, 1998.

SimpsonScarborough. "Higher Ed and COVID-19 National Student Survey Part III—The Fragility of Trust." August 2020.

"Six Fun Games to Help You Talk about End-of-Life Care." The Conversation Project, November 11, 2019. https://theconversationproject.org/tcp -blog/death-is-not-a-game-well-sometimes-it-is.

Sonious, David. *Divided We Fall.* New York: Page, 2017.

Sonmez, Felicia. "Texas Lt. Gov. Dan Patrick Comes under Fire for Saying Seniors Should 'Take a Chance' on Their Own Lives for Sake of Grandchildren during Coronavirus Crisis." *Washington Post,* March 24, 2020.

Stein, Marc. "Led by N.B.A., Boycotts Disrupt Pro Sports in Wake of Blake Shooting." *New York Times,* August 29, 2020.

Strauss, Valerie. "N.C. Governor Attacks Higher Ed, Proposes Funding Colleges by Graduates' Jobs." *Washington Post,* February 7, 2013.

Svrluga, Susan. "Scores of College Presidents Urge Education Department to Stop Its Investigation of Princeton." *Washington Post,* September 25, 2020.

Tokarczyk, Melissa. "Hidden Anxieties of the White Working Class." *Working Class Perspectives,* December 19, 2016.

Toynbee, Arnold, et al., eds. *Changing Attitudes toward Death in the Modern Western World.* New York: McGraw Hill, 1968.

Treisman, Rachel. "The NFL Will Play 'Lift Every Voice and Sing' before Each Season Opener Game." NPR, July 2, 2020. Audio.

Trump, Donald. "Nevada Caucus Victory Speech." February 23, 2016. http://www.qz.com.

———. "Remarks by President Trump at Signing of Executive Order, Improving Free Inquiry, Transparency, and Accountability at Colleges and Universities.'" March 21, 2019. http://www.whitehouse.gov.

Trusted Decision Maker. https://www.instituteforhumancaring.org /Advance-Care-Planning.aspx.

Twain, Mark. *Notebook.* New York: Cooper Square, 1908. Google Books.

Wallace, Jeremy. "Rick Scott No Fan of Anthropology." *Sarasota Herald-Tribune,* October 10, 2011.

Watkins, Ali, Michael Rothfeld, William K. Rashbaum, and Brian M. Rosenthal. "Top E.R. Doctor Who Treated Virus Patients Dies by Suicide." *New York Times,* April 27, 2020.

Wibby, Chuck. "From the Editorial Advisory Board: 'Liberal' Not Always Political." *Colorado Daily Camera,* June 29, 2018.

Will, George. "On American Campuses, Freedom from Speech." *Washington Post,* November 13, 2015.

Wines, Michael, and Aishvarya Kavi. "March on Washington 2020: Protesters Hope to Rekindle Spirit of 1963." *New York Times,* August 28, 2020.

Van Zyl, Carin, and Dawn M. Gross. "For People Dying to Talk, It Finally Pays to Listen with Reimbursable Advance Care Planning." *AMA Journal of Ethics,* August 2018.